Diary of a Journey to Abyssinia, 1868

Diary of a Journey to Abyssinia, 1868

With the Expedition under Sir Robert Napier, K.C.S.I.

The Diary and Observations
of

William Simpson

of the *Illustrated London News*

Edited and annotated by

Richard Pankhurst

With introductions by Richard Pankhurst,
Peter Harrington and Frederic A. Sharf

Based on the manuscript in the collection of
Jean S. and Frederic A. Sharf
Chestnut Hill, Mass., U.S.A.

TSEHAI
Publishers and Distributors

Diary of a Journey
to Abyssinia, 1868

Copyright © 2002 by Frederic A. Sharf. All rights Reserved.

This book is published in celebration of the
Sixth International Conference on the History of Ethiopian Art,
5 to 8 November 2002 Institute of Ethiopian Studies, Addis Ababa, Ethiopia.

Publication is made possible by the cooperation of
Frederic A. Sharf and Richard Pankhurst.

Tsehai books may be purchased for educational, business, or sales promotional use. For
information please contact Mekdes Taye at our Marketing Department.

Published by Tsehai Publishers and Institute of Ethiopian Studies.

Tsehai Publishers and Distributors
P. O. Box: 1881, Hollywood, CA 90078
www.tsehaipublishers.com • email: tsehaipublishers@juno.com

Publisher: Elias Wondimu
Book Design: Paul Cyr and Cynthia Brown, Newburyport Press Inc., MA
Copy Editor: Nancy TenBroeck

Library of Congress Catalog Card Number: 2002110315
ISBN: 0-9723172-1-x

FIRST EDITION: November 2002

10 9 8 7 6 5 4 3 2 1 0

Printed by Newburyport Press Inc. in the United States of America
www.newburyportpress.com

ınformatıon about the authors

RICHARD PANKHURST is a scholar and educator who has lived in Ethiopia for more than thirty years. He currently serves as Professor at the Institute of Ethiopian Studies in Addis Ababa. In addition to the numerous books and articles listed in the Bibliography, a recent work is *The Ethiopians: A History* (1998) in the series "The Peoples of Africa."

PETER HARRINGTON, Curator of the Anne S. K. Brown Military Collection at Brown University, Providence, Rhode Island, is the author of *British Artists and War.* He is the co-author (with Frederic Sharf) of *"A Splendid Little War:" The Spanish-American War, 1898; Omdurman, 1898: The Eyewitnesses Speak; The Boxer Rebellion: China, 1900—The Artists' Perspective;* and *China, 1900: The Eyewitnesses Speak.*

FREDERIC A. SHARF is a scholar and collector who specializes in art, photography, and unpublished manuscript material relating to wars fought during the several decades before and after 1900. He is a resident of Chestnut Hill, Massachusetts.

☙

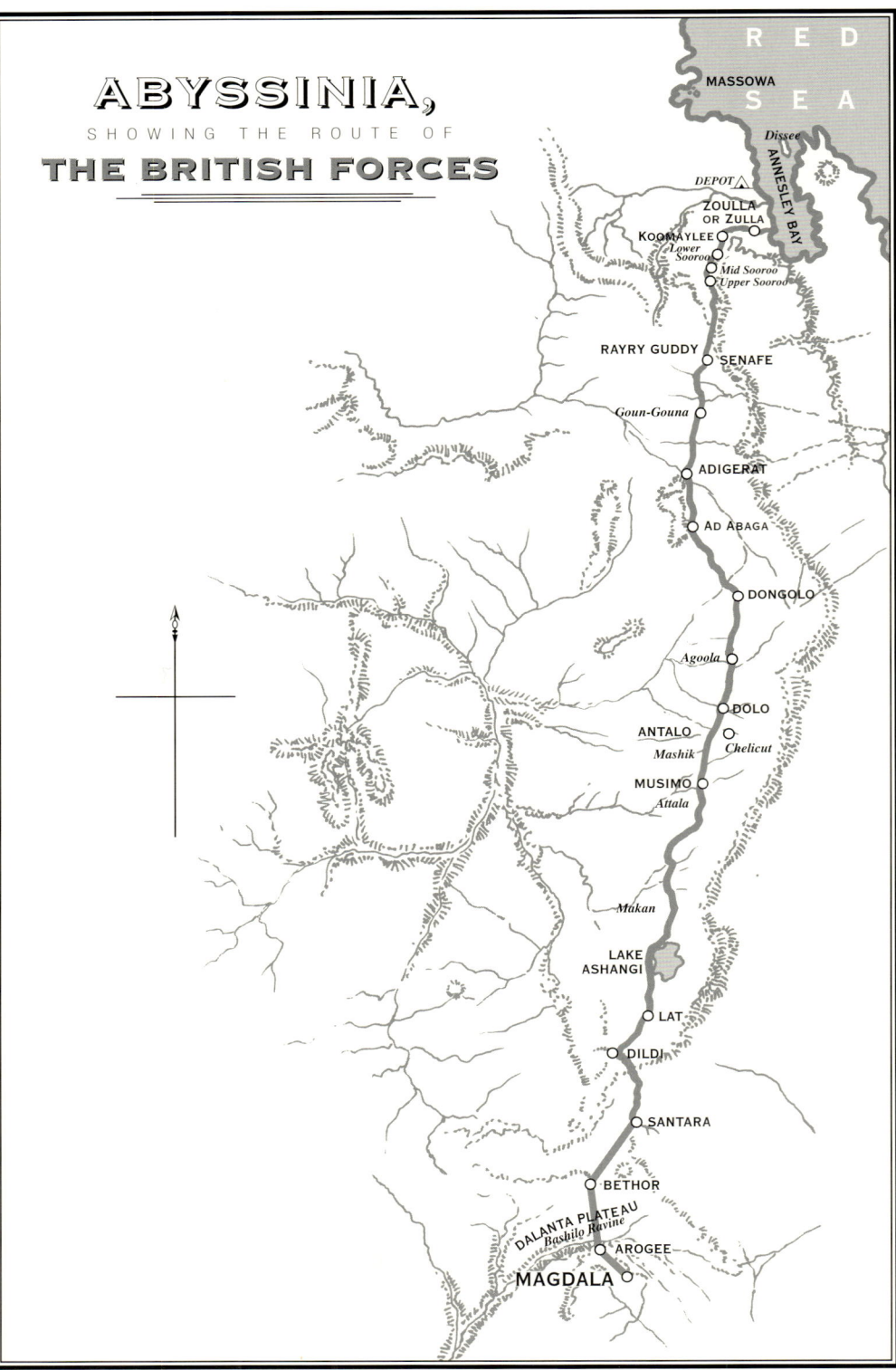

contents

DIARY OF A JOURNEY TO ABYSSINIA BY WILLIAM SIMPSON
THE OUTWARD JOURNEY:

THE RETURN WITH EXPEDITION FORCES:

APPENDIXES:

GENERAL INFORMATION:

The most authoritative source on the 1868 Expedition is the account written soon afterwards by Messrs. Holland and Hozier. The reader may consult this work for additional information about the places visited and the personalities encountered by William Simpson.

The following abbreviations have been used in crediting frequently used sources (see the Bibliography for full publication information).

H&H, *Record*	Trevenen J. Holland and Henry M. Hozier, *Record of the Expedition to Abyssinia*
Autobiography	William Simpson, *The Autobiography of William Simpson, R.I.*
"Jottings"	William Simpson, "An Artist's Jottings in Abyssinia."
ILN	Articles by William Simpson in *Illustrated London News* (1868)

Simpson generally wrote in his diary at the end of the day, and thus his location then is given with the date.

For the convenience of the reader, occasional spelling mistakes in the narrative have been corrected (i.e., "their" for "there" and names of individuals and places); and punctuation has been added in a few cases. Place names were casually spelled at the time and have been standardized here. Definitions of unfamiliar words have been added [in brackets].

SEE ALSO THE FOLLOWING APPENDIXES:
  C: British Military Officers Mentioned in Text (first mention noted with *);
  D: List of distances for march of each day (with alternate spellings of place names);
  E. British and Indian Units in Campaign.

LiST OF iLLUSTRATiONS

These illustrations were based on art work by William Simpson; they accompanied articles which he sent to the *Illustrated London News*.

Review of the British Army at the Queen's Birthday, Senafe [25 May]

FOREWORD

by Frederic A. Sharf

In October 1999 I was fortunate enough to have the opportunity to acquire the original manuscript diary kept by William Simpson on his trip to Abyssinia in 1868. It had descended in the family along with other diaries and sketch books, most of which have now been dispersed into appropriate libraries in Great Britain and the United States.

It was always my intention to make this diary available to the public by having the manuscript transcribed and edited for publication. I was very fortunate that the noted Ethiopian scholar RICHARD PANKHURST was equally interested in such an undertaking; without his involvement and his personal commitment of time the publication would never have been possible.

From the start, my friend and colleague PETER HARRINGTON, a noted military historian and curator of the Anne S. K. Brown Military Collection at Brown University in Providence, Rhode Island, has been intimately involved. He has long had a keen interest in Simpson, and several original Simpson items reside in the collection of which he is curator.

A great deal of painstaking research lies behind this publication. I was fortunate to have enthusiastic support in this research from GLENN MITCHELL, who runs the military department of Maggs Bros. Ltd. in London. He has been tireless in his efforts to track down numerous British military men mentioned by Simpson in the Diary.

Access to the archives of the *Illustrated London New*s was arranged by Ms. Alison Booth, Editor, The Illustrated London News Group, London, England. Research accommodation and photocopy services were arranged by Richard Pitkin, Archivist of The Illustrated London News Group, London.

Access to drawings in the collection of the National Army Museum, London, England was arrranged by Ms. Emily Davis.

General advice and support has been provided by William T. La Moy, James Duncan Phillips Librarian of the Peabody Essex Museum, Salem, Massachusetts, USA.

Lastly, I must express my appreciation to Nancy TenBroeck for her editorial help in pulling the pieces together.

For all of us, this has been a labor of love and a chance to add another resource to the scholarly world. Our hope is that this publication will find a home in libraries around the world and will be useful to scholars now and in the future.

Frederic A. Sharf
August 2002

PREFACE:

ᴛʜᴇ ᴀʀᴛɪsᴛɪᴄ ᴀsᴘᴇᴄᴛs ᴏꜰ ᴛʜᴇ ᴀʙʏssɪɴɪᴀɴ ᴇxᴘᴇᴅɪᴛɪᴏɴ

by Frederic A. Sharf

On 3 March 1868, the journalist and artist William Simpson left London to join the British Expedition to Abyssinia. He was dispatched on this lengthy journey by the *Illustrated London News*. It is logical to question their reasons for sending him on such a long and arduous trip, and at such a late date.

The *ILN* had given extensive coverage to the British Expedition into Abyssinia for the previous five months. They had been relying on reports from various freelance men with varying degrees of literary and artistic competence—these ranged from professional journalists such as George Henty to professional adventurers like Henry Astbury Leveson (known as "The Old Shekarry").

However the primary source of images and text in Abyssinia was the army officers who were part of the Expedition. Once again, there was a wide range of such men; but for the most part they were officers in the Indian Army, and predominantly officers in the Bombay Staff Corps. (An exception was the contributions from the Prussian Military Attaché, Count [Graf] von Seckendorff, who was attached to Napier's Headquarters and who submitted very accomplished drawings.)

The most important regular source of Abyssinian images was Major Robert Baigrie, whose identity (for some unknown reason) was kept secret until the very end of the campaign. Baigrie had the advantage of being among the initial group of British officers to arrive in Abyssinia on 4 October 1867. He was a member of the Reconnoitring Expedition whose job it was to find the best route for an army and its supplies to go from Annesley Bay to Magdala. The *Illustrated London News* was able to publish his first eyewitness drawings from

1

Abyssinia on 30 November 1867; Baigrie was identified simply as a "Staff Officer."

Baigrie supplied text to accompany each of his drawings; this was usually written on the reverse of the drawing itself. His submissions appeared frequently from 30 November onwards. He was a talented topographical draftsman; his drawings were designed for military purposes, producing images which could be used by the army to calculate how to move a large army across a very inhospitable landscape. However a comment by the editors of the *ILN* in their issue of 8 February provides an important clue about why they decided to send Simpson when they praise "our valued correspondent the Staff Officer" for his skill in "sketching the scenery of the Abyssinian frontier." They needed more human interest; Simpson's assignment was specifically to provide images of people and their lifestyles.

It was quite common during the 19th century and even into the 20th century for publishers to send so-called "special correspondents" to distant places on short notice. However Simpson's journey does not seem to fall into this category because he had enough advance warning to equip himself with some high-powered letters of introduction. This leads me to speculate that he was notified of this assignment in mid-February of 1868 and had several weeks in which to prepare for the journey.

Having considered sending Simpson, the editors certainly based their decision on information from telegraphic sources. Napier's staff provided the Foreign Office and the War Office with continuous updates, which were then released to the press. The *ILN* of 8 February 1868 contains two such reports; the first stated that the road from the seacoast to Senafe was open, enabling the army to move supplies to the camp at Senafe; and another (dated 28 January) announced that Napier would soon begin to move his army towards Antalo. Thus it was clear that the real action in Abyssinia was going to take place in the near future; particularly since Napier would need to move his army quickly enough to reach Magdala, defeat Theodore, and return to the coast before May, when the rainy season began.

Simpson could be expected to reach Napier's Headquarters within six to eight weeks, and would thus be in time to witness the fall of Magdala, predicted for the end of April. His employers realized that once he got to Abyssinia he could travel on his own at two or three times the speed of an army, and they could thus assume that he would get to the front much faster than the army could travel. Having dispatched Simpson to the front, the *ILN* continued to rely on Baigrie and other army officers for images.

However an interesting new source of images opened up to them when they received the first of a series of actual photographs taken by the Royal Engineers—for example, a panoramic three-part photo of the Zoulla base camp, which was published on 14 March. Such images would seem to have been a very promising source of illustrations; but in fact, no other photographic image was published. We do not know the reason.

The presence of trained photographers in the Abyssinian Expedition Force was a significant innovation. It was probably the first time in history that a military expedition included this kind of official team. The Duke of Cambridge, who was Commander-in-Chief of the British army, forwarded a recommendation from the Director of the Royal Engineer Establishment to the Secretary of State for India, calling for the establishment of this team. It was quickly approved on 18 September, and a team of seven men was assembled. The leader was Sergeant John Harrold, and the other six men had received special photographic training. They were attached to the 10th Company of Royal Engineers, under the command of Major Gordon Douglas Pritchard.

The photo team left London on 4 November 1867; their arrival at Annesley Bay was recorded in an official dispatch dated 7 December. Soon they began work, making photos of plans, views, surveys of routes, and documenting the engineering/organization results which were essential to preparations for the campaign. Before the campaign ended, this team produced 15,200 prints, all mounted on linen. Once the actual march to Magdala commenced, the photographers and the signallers marched with the First Brigade, and thus were at the very forefront of the action.[i-1]

Simpson's drawings of people and places turned out to be incredibly important in conveying to Western audiences some sense of the reality of this country— one which few Westerners had ever visited. And the *ILN* used the Simpson material long after it was known in England that Magdala had capitulated. The first telegraphed news came to London on Sunday, 26 April and appeared in the *ILN* issue of Saturday, 2 May. Ironically, Simpson's first sketch appeared in the *ILN* on 9 May, a week after his audience knew of the fall of Magdala; but his art work continued to be published during the months of May through August 1868.[i-2] Finally on 5 September the editors included the last illustrations drawn from his sketches, announcing that "We now conclude the series of illustrations of the late British expedition in Abyssinia...."

The Abyssinian Expedition suffered from an inherent problem: seven months of preparation were required, and there was only one week of action. Perhaps this partly explains why Simpson spent so much of his time and attention in depicting and trying to understand the Coptic church. With no military action to report—he arrived too late to witness even the one week of action—he was fortunate to have a strong ethnographic interest which instinctively led him to a unique aspect of Abyssinia which he felt would resonate with a Victorian English audience.

INTRODUCTION:

THE BRITISH EXPEDITION TO MAGDALA:
ITS CAUSES AND CONSEQUENCES

by Richard Pankhurst

THE ORIGINS AND BACKGROUND

The origins of the British expedition to Magdala (known in Ethiopia as Maqdala or Mäqdäla) had their roots in the critical state of early nineteenth century Ethiopian society. The old Christian state, with its capital at Gondar in the north-west of the land, was seriously in decline. The centralising power of the monarchy had collapsed, and a succession of emperors had been reduced to the status of mere puppets, controlled by one feudal lord or another. The principal provinces—Tegray, Bagemder, Gojjam and Shawa—had all come under the control of virtually independent chiefs. Civil war between these rulers was common, and their armies, swollen in numbers through decades of fighting, often ravaged the peasantry, spreading misery and desolation wherever they went. As a consequence, the standard of living in many areas was in decline and culture was imperiled.[ii-1]

Ethiopia suffered from disunity and civil war at the very moment when the outside world was involved in the Industrial Revolution. This great transformation in technology, which was accompanied by immense advances in armaments as well as in transport, communications and medicine, had first manifested itself in Western Europe in the late eighteenth and early nineteenth centuries, and soon had major implications for other continents. Technological progress was symbolised by the steamboat, the railway, and faster-firing rifles, and it facilitated overseas expansion by Britain and France. This led to occupation by the British of the port of Aden in 1839, and the almost simultaneous landing of the French on the southern Red Sea coast of Africa.

As the advance of modern technology began to spread to other lands, one of the first African countries to be affected was Ethiopia's northern neighbour, Egypt. Taking advantage of its new economic and military power, that country's rulers embarked on a policy of extensive territorial expansion. This took the Egyptians southwards into the Sudan and along the coast of the Red Sea. To the alarm of the rulers of Ethiopia, the Egyptian khedive then began annexing Ethiopia's northern and western borderlands—which was the more serious in that it threatened the country's access to the sea.

By the middle of the nineteenth century it was clearly evident that Ethiopia, to maintain its territorial integrity as well as to benefit from the new inventions in technology, had to embark on a policy of modernisation. This, in the Ethiopian context, could be achieved only through unification and centralisation—processes which, it may be recalled, at that time had not yet been achieved in either Germany or Italy—which could be accomplished only by a strong ruler, able to crush all rival warlords and make himself the undisputed master of the country.

Such a task, given the mountainous nature of the country and the Ethiopian people's pride in their age-old independence, could not easily be achieved—and was not in fact carried out until well after the time covered in this volume.

THE RISE OF THEODORE (OR TÉWODROS)

The struggle between Ethiopian warlords, from which the country had been suffering for over a hundred years, culminated around the middle of the century in the advent of Emperor Téwodros II, then better known in Britain as Theodore, who is in a sense the central figure in our story.

The Emperor had begun his career as a little-known rebel, but had rapidly fought his way to the throne.[ii-2] He proved to be a charismatic leader who impressed European contemporaries by his Messianic sense of purpose, and by his unbending determination to maintain his country's independence and restore its greatness—which was to make him, posthumously, a hero for many Ethiopian patriots.

INTRODUCTION: CAUSES AND CONSEQUENCES

He was crowned on 7 February 1855, and adopted the name of Téwodros. This was significant because an old prophecy, then widely believed throughout the land, held that a king of that name would one day come, rule righteously, and capture Jerusalem.

Theodore, a unique figure in Ethiopian history, won the immediate admiration of the then British Consul, Walter Plowden. Referring to the newly-crowned ruler only a couple of months later, on 25 April 1855, he observed that Theodore considered himself a "destined monarch" and added:

> The King is capable of great things, good or evil. He wishes to discipline his army, and has in part already succeeded; to abolish the feudal system; to have paid Governors and Judges; and to disarm the people. He is just, hearing in person the poorest peasant; he has stopped the system of bribes; he has by his own example, and by giving dowries and rewards to those who marry, discouraged polygamy and concubinage, and has tranquilized the whole country....[ii-3]

In a report on 25 June, Plowden further described the monarch's personality, which was to impinge materially on the story told in the following pages:

> The king is young in years, vigorous in all manly exercises, of a striking countenance, particularly polite and engaging when pleased, and mostly displaying great tact and delicacy. He is persuaded that he is destined to restore the glories of Ethiopian Empire, and to achieve great conquests; of untiring energy, both mental and bodily, his personal and moral daring are boundless. The latter is well proved by his severity towards his soldiers, even when these, pressed by hunger, are mutinous, and he is in front of powerful foes; more so even by pressing reforms in a country so little used to any yoke, whilst engaged in unceasing hostilities, and his suppression of the power of the great feudal chiefs at a moment when any inferior man would have sought to conciliate them as the stepping-stones to Empire.

> When aroused [*Plowden continues*] his wrath is terrible, and all tremble; but at all moments he is in perfect self-command. Indefatigable in business, he takes little repose night or day; his ideas and language are

clear and precise; hesitation is not known to him; and he has neither councilors nor go-betweens. He is fond of splendour and receives in state even on a campaign. He is unsparing in punishment....He is generous to excess, and free from all cupidity, regarding nothing with pleasure or desire but munitions of war for his soldiers. He has hitherto exercised the utmost clemency towards the vanquished, treating them rather as his friends than his enemies. His faith is signal; 'without Christ,' he says, 'I am nothing; if He has destined me to purify and reform this distracted kingdom, with His aid who can stay me?'—nay, sometimes he is on the point of not caring for human assistance at all.

Elaborating further on the monarch's character, Plowden observed, significantly in the light of later events, that the Ethiopian monarch was

particularly jealous....of his sovereign rights, and of anything that appears to trench upon them; he wishes, in a short time, to send embassies to the Great European Powers to treat with them on equal terms. The most difficult trait of his character is this jealousy and the pride, fed by ignorance, that renders it impossible for him to believe that so great a monarch as himself exists in the world.

Turning, finally, to the young Emperor's ambitions, Plowden concluded:

The arduous task of breaking the power of the great feudal Chiefs—a task achieved in Europe only during the reign of many consecutive kings—he has commenced by chaining almost all who were dangerous, avowing his intention of liberating them when his power shall be consolidated. He has placed the soldiers of the different provinces under the command of his own trusted followers, to whom he has given high titles, but no power to judge or punish; thus, in fact, creating generals in place of feudal chieftains more proud of their birth than of their monarch, and organising a new nobility, a legion of honour dependent on himself, and chosen for their daring and fidelity.

....Some of his ideas may be imperfect, others impracticable, but a man who has done so much and contemplates such giant designs cannot be regarded as of ordinary stamp.[ii-4]

INTRODUCTION: CAUSES AND CONSEQUENCES

Theodore's overriding objective, we may comment, was to unify the country under his absolute rule. To this end he built up an army said to number over 150,000 men,[ii-5] and undertook a series of military expeditions to Tegray, Gondar, Wallo and Shawa. This brought most of historic Ethiopia under his nominal control, at least temporarily. His overall position was, however, extremely difficult, and it proved to be untenable. His power base, situated around his capital at Dabra Tabor in the north-west of the country, was far away from the coast, through which firearms were imported; and to which his rivals, the rulers of Tegray and Shawa, had far better access than he.

Deeply conscious of the impossibility of his position, and of the need to increase his military strength, he was determined to reform and modernise his empire. He sought, as Plowden reports, to abolish the old feudal levies, whose soldiers lived by looting the countryside, and to replace them by a trained (and as far as possible, regularly paid) army directly loyal to himself. This was no easy task, for he was unable to raise sufficient taxes to pay his troops, who were thus often obliged to continue their practice of rapine. He was so pained by this, his chronicle states, that he on one occasion cursed his men, declaring, "Soldiers, as you have killed [the cattle] which belongs to the poor, so may God do unto you!"[ii-6] At other times, however, he is reported to have despatched trusted officers to protect the peasants from the excesses of his own soldiers, and announced his intention, in Biblical terms, to "convert swords and spears into plough-shares, and cause the plough-ox to be sold dearer than the noblest war-horse."[ii-7]

Realising the overwhelming importance of technological innovation and above all the necessity of acquiring modern firearms, in 1855 he accepted an offer from Samuel Gobat, the Anglican Bishop of Jerusalem, to send a group of young Protestant missionary craftsmen. They had received their training at the St. Chrischona Institute, near Basle, Switzerland, and were trained in technical as well as religious fields. Theodore welcomed these missionaries warmly, settled them on the hill of Gafat, near to his capital at Dabra Tabor, and immediately put them to work on the crafts in which they were skilled.[ii-8]

Preoccupied by his over-riding desire for firearms, he shortly afterwards asked them to assist him in an entirely new activity: cannon-making. They replied that they had "neither knowledge nor experience" of that work. Theodore refused, however, to take no for an answer. "If you are my friends," he declared, "try. If God allows the work to succeed, it will be well. If not, it will also be well!" To underline his insistence on being obeyed, however, he arrested the missionaries' servants.

Understanding that there could be no trifling with their strong-willed taskmaster, the craftsmen had no option but to obey his wishes. After many fruitless efforts at metal casting, they eventually succeeded. One of the leading missionaries, Theophilus Waldmeier, recalls that, after "unspeakable effort, we made a final despairing attempt...and, behold, for the first time we were successful...The King was pleased beyond all measure with our little piece of metal, kissed it, and cried, 'Now I am convinced that it is possible to make everything in Habash [i.e. Abyssinia]. Praise and thanks be to Him for it.'"**ii-9**

The need to transport his artillery from one part of the country to another caused Theodore also to become Ethiopia's first road-builder. "From early dawn to late at night," recalls the foreign doctor Henry Blanc, the innovating monarch was "hard at work" on the roads. "With his own hands he removed the stones, levelled the ground, or helped to fill up ravines. No one could leave so long as he was there himself; no one would think of eating, or of rest, while the Emperor showed the example and shared the hardships."**ii-10**

Though primarily concerned with military and related matters, he also attempted to carry out other reforms. He thus sought to abolish the slave trade; to reduce the then very extensive church holdings of land (a reform which created strong opposition from the Church); and to promote the written use of the vernacular tongue (Amharic) in place of the old classical language (Ge'ez), which—like Latin in Europe—was largely dead.

THEODORE'S DISPUTE WITH THE BRITISH GOVERNMENT

Theodore's attempts at unification and reform, and his confrontation with many enemies among the provincial nobility and priesthood, led inexorably but unnecessarily—and in some ways entirely unexpectedly—to a dispute with the British government. This in turn brought the British Expedition to the Emperor's mountain fortress of Magdala—the remarkable military enterprise which forms the subject of Simpson's diary.

To understand the paradoxical character of this dispute one should recall that the by then sorely-pressed Ethiopian monarch had earlier enjoyed the close friendship of two Englishmen, the above-mentioned Consul Plowden, whom he considered as his principal foreign adviser, and John Bell, whom he appointed as his Chancellor. Both—perhaps to please their master—had assured him of British friendship for his country, and he seems to have accepted their expressions of support at face value. Though they had both subsequently died, he reportedly remembered them with affection.[ii-11]

Confronted meanwhile with increasing Egyptian-Ottoman incursions at the coast, Theodore decided, on 29 October 1862, to despatch a friendly letter to Queen Victoria. In it he recalled that he had been told—presumably by Plowden and Bell—that she was "a great Christian queen," who "loved Christians." He therefore announced his desire to send her an embassy; but having been prevented from doing so by the Egyptians at the coast, he inquired how he could send her presents, and ended his letter by appealing to her to "stand by him," a fellow Christian, in the face of a threatened attack by Muslim Egypt, then a part of the Ottoman Empire.[ii-12]

The Emperor gave this letter to Plowden's successor, Consul Duncan Cameron, whom he asked to take it to Britain. He also made several oral requests. In particular, he asked Britain to prevent the incursion of the Turkish-Ottoman fleet off the Ethiopian coast; to help him purchase firearms; and to provide him with an engineer to build roads.[ii-13]

Theodore's letter, couched in terms reminiscent of the medieval Crusades, would a few centuries earlier have been enthusiastically welcomed by European Christendom which sought an alliance with the Ethiopian Kingdom of Prester John, against the Saracens.[ii-14] However the Emperor's words evoked little sympathy from the more commercially-minded British government of the mid-nineteenth century. Britain was by then keenly interested in Egyptian cotton, upon which the mills of Lancashire depended, and which was the more important in that cotton was in short supply on account of the American Civil War. Moreover the Ottoman Empire, of which

INTRODUCTION: CAUSES AND CONSEQUENCES

Egypt still formed a part, though a largely independent one, was regarded by the British government as a useful buttress against the expansion of Russia—which they saw as a potential threat to the British Empire in India. Britain had therefore no wish to alienate either Egypt or the Ottoman Empire by befriending—or offering protection to—Ethiopia, whose borderlands they were then annexing. The Emperor's letter was accordingly forwarded by the Foreign Office to the India Office, where it was merely filed, and left unanswered.

Six months or so later, on 22 April 1863, the British Foreign Secretary, Earl Russell, added insult to injury. He informed Consul Cameron that the British government, not wishing to be embroiled in Ethiopian affairs, no longer wanted a British Consul in the country. Cameron was accordingly told to withdraw to the Red Sea port of Massawa.[ii-15]

Theodore, for his part, was facing increasingly serious difficulties from rebels in the interior, as well as from the Egyptians at the coast and in the Sudan. He was therefore in even greater need of the assistance for which he had appealed in his letter to Queen Victoria.

A proud man, who was exceedingly conscious of his own dignity and importance, as Plowden had earlier noted, the Emperor was not amused by the British government's continued failure to answer his letter. Moreover, he was disquieted by the (to his mind) inexplicable failure of Britain, which he regarded as his natural ally, to communicate with Ethiopia, a fellow Christian country. His displeasure was heightened by the news that Cameron, to whom he had entrusted his letter, had not taken it to the coast himself, but merely entrusted it to a servant. It later transpired that the Consul had been visiting the Egyptian rulers on Ethiopia's western frontier.[ii-16] He had done so apparently quite honourably in an attempt to curtail the slave trade in that area, but his exchange of courtesies with the Egyptian authorities appeared to the Ethiopian monarch as fraternisation with his enemies, the invaders of his country.

Not long after this the Emperor learnt that Henry Stern, a by no means humble Protestant missionary, had written a book, *Wanderings among the Falashas,* in which he alleged that Theodore's mother had been so poor that she had been obliged to sell *kosso*, the traditional Ethiopian cure for tapeworm.[ii-17] Questioned about this act of laisse-majesté, which seemed calculated to undermine the Emperor's international image, about which Theodore felt strongly, the missionary had placed his finger to his mouth in a gesture which was interpreted as one of defiance. The Emperor, deeply angered, ordered him to be whipped.

Further evidence of a British shift of policy at Ethiopia's expense reached Theodore shortly afterwards. He was informed that the Egyptian Coptic priests in Jerusalem had seized an Ethiopian convent, and that whereas the previous British representative there, Consul James Finn, had protected the Ethiopian community from victimisation, his successor, Consul Noel Moore, had declared himself powerless to act without instructions from his superiors, who were unwilling to intervene.

Theodore was deeply disturbed by this news; and probably aware that Cameron was under orders to leave the country, responded by placing him in chains. The imprisonment, which in Britain seemed a gross violation of the immunity traditionally accorded in Europe to diplomatic envoys, was less surprising in the Ethiopian context—where messengers were considered of little consequence and where high-ranking dignitaries, and even members of the royal family, were often kept in detention.

The act did, however, finally remind the British government that it had not answered the Emperor's letter. A friendly reply was therefore hastily drawn up. This was entrusted to Hormuzd Rassam, the British Assistant Resident in Aden, who reached Theodore's camp in 1866, almost half a decade after the despatch of Theodore's first letter. The Emperor welcomed him graciously, but shortly afterwards ordered that he too be placed in detention, apparently in the hope that by holding Cameron, Rassam and others as hostages he would force the British government, which he probably still regarded as his potential friend, to inquire into the matter, and in particular to send him craftsmen of whose skills he was in urgent need.

Although appearing to the British government as well-nigh unforgivably high-handed, this action almost had the result its author wished. The Foreign Office agreed to recruit the artisans Theodore had demanded and even went so far as to despatch them to the port of Massawa. However by then the British mistrusted Theodore's intentions and had grown tired of seemingly interminable negotiations with the Emperor. They were under persistent pressure from the families of the captives—as well as from the press—and feared that the Ethiopian ruler might be seeking to exploit his possession of an increasing number of Europeans to extract ever further concessions.

The British government therefore refused to allow the workmen to go to the Emperor's capital until his captives were actually released. Theodore, equally unbending, declared himself unwilling to free the prisoners until the arrival of the artisans at his camp. Negotiations had thus reached a deadlock.

THE NAPIER EXPEDITION

By the summer of 1866 the British government had become more and more frustrated by Theodore's imprisonment of its nationals and other Europeans. This seemingly insolent behaviour in relation to the "captives" was regarded not only as a "grave outrage and insult" to Victorian England, but also as a threat to British prestige in India and the East.

Though slow to act, the British government was increasingly inclined to the use of force. This attitude was reinforced in official circles by an awareness that Theodore's power was collapsing on account of increasing rebellion, and that his writ extended hardly farther than the location of his army. With reports of this deterioration, and after much discussion, the British government finally decided on 13 August 1867 that the captives should be liberated by force of arms. An ultimatum was duly despatched to Theodore on 9 September.

Confronted with the threat of British invasion, the Emperor burnt down his capital at Dabra Tabor on 10 October, and began a long march, with all his artillery, to the seemingly impregnable mountain fortress of Magdala, where his European captives were to spend their last months of imprisonment. This journey took no less than six months and was extremely difficult, for the Emperor had in places to excavate or build a road over which to drag his cannons and mortars.

INTRODUCTION: CAUSES AND CONSEQUENCES

The British government decided to entrust its "Abyssinian Expedition" to an able British officer with experience of China and the East. This was Sir Robert Napier, who had been Commander-in-Chief of the Bombay Army in India since 1865. Studying how best to effect the captives' liberation he rejected the idea, then widely circulated, of a "rapid dash" by a small commando-like band of highly-armed men, in favour of marching to Magdala with a sizable army capable of holding its own in potentially hostile territory. His plans were accepted by the British government, with the result that he eventually had at his disposal an expeditionary army of no less than 62,220 men and 36,094 animals. The fighting force itself comprised 13,088 troops, of whom 4,038 were Europeans and 9,050 were Indians.

The decision to dispatch an Anglo-Indian—and predominantly Indian—force meant that the Expedition was heterogeneous both in composition and armament. The British troops carried breech-loading rifles, before then not used in warfare, as well as the most modern types of artillery and another innovation: rockets. They also brought supplies for a field telegraph, a short railway which would run 12 miles inland from the coast, water condensers for use by the sea, and well-drilling equipment to be employed in the interior. The Indian troops, on the other hand, were far less well-equipped. They carried the old smooth-bore, muzzle-loading muskets, not so different from those in use by the Emperor's troops. Considerable diversity was also apparent in the clothing: some soldiers were outfitted in the newly-introduced khaki uniforms, while others wore traditional red coats dating back to earlier wars.

Transportation for these troops was provided by forty-four elephants, 5,735 camels, 17,943 mules and ponies, 8,075 bullocks, and 2,538 horses, all shipped in for the occasion. The expeditionary force also utilised 75 steamers, 205 sailing vessels, and 11 smaller craft. The total cost was close to £450,000 per month.

On 21 October 1867 the British advance guard landed in the Bay of Zoulla—then often referred to in British circles as Annesley Bay—south of Massawa. The site had been chosen in agreement with the Egyptians, who claimed authority over most of the Red Sea coast of Africa and were reluctant to make the port of Massawa available for the expedition. Napier himself landed at Zoulla on 2 January of the following year, and began the main march inland, towards Magdala, twenty-three days later. By 29 January he was at Senafe, which became one of the Expedition's main headquarters, while the advance guard had by then moved 35 miles further on to Adigerat.

Meeting no resistance, but having to traverse extremely rugged countryside and suffering at times from acute shortage of both food and water, the British advance guard proceeded to Antalo, 200 miles from the coast, on 14 February. Eleven days later the Commander-in-Chief held a notable meeting with Dajazmach Kasa, the ruler of Tegray,[ii-18] who, as a strong opponent of Theodore, promised the British his full co-operation. A no less auspicious meeting took place with Wagshum Gobazé, the ruler of Lasta,[ii-19] who was another implacable enemy of Theodore, on 30 March.

These two meetings, and the agreements concluded at them, were important in that they ensured that the Expedition was able to cross most of northern Ethiopia—right up to the gates of Magdala, where the Emperor was by then encamped—without encountering any armed opposition whatsoever. The campaign was thus reduced from the invasion of an entire country, as it had at one point appeared, to the capture of a single mountain which was defended by perhaps 4,000 men, of whom only 3,000 had firearms.

Fighting did not begin until Good Friday, 10 April, when the British were within sight of Theodore's capital. The Ethiopians were then at the end of their strict Lenten fast. They were commanded by one of the Emperor's most loyal chiefs, Fitawrari Gabriyé. Looking down from their mountain stronghold, they saw their much more numerous enemy from above; but undeterred, they charged down the mountain into the nearby Arogee plain. There they were confronted by massed British artillery. Clements Markham recalls,

> The Snider rifles kept up a fire which no Abyssinian troops could stand. They were mown down in lines, and unable to get within range them-selves. Hope left them. Led on by their gallant old General....they returned again and again to charge with great bravery. But it was like a man struggling against machinery—the most heroic courage could do nothing in the face of such vast inequality of arms.

Gabriyé and most of the officers of the Ethiopian forces were killed. Further fighting took place at the nearby Dam-wanz ravine, where Theodore's men advanced "with extraordinary gallantry" until they were finally repelled. The area was soon "choked with dead," and the stream at the bottom "ran with blood."[ii-20]

Early on the following day, Saturday 11 April, Theodore, realising the magnitude of his defeat, attempted to sue for peace. He sent two of the British prisoners down to Napier's camp, with a message to the effect that he desired to be "reconciled with the English," but, Markham observes, the victorious Commander-in-Chief could offer "no terms short of unconditional surrender." The two prisoners were accordingly sent back to the Emperor with a written message from Napier, stating:

> Your Majesty has fought like a brave man, and has been overcome by the superior power of the British army. It is my desire that no more blood may be shed. If, therefore, Your Majesty will submit to the Queen of England, and bring all the Europeans now in your Majesty's hands into the British camp, I guarantee honourable treatment for yourself and all the members of your Majesty's family.[ii-21]

When this letter reached him Theodore was engaged in dictating a kind of last testament to the Ethiopian people. He interrupted his thoughts, however, to reply to the British.

In a remarkable text, Theodore began by chiding his men for their defeat, and asked, "O people of Abyssinia! Will it always be thus that you flee before the enemy when I myself, by the power of God, go not forth with you to encourage you?"

Later in the text, he turned to the British, conceding that God had given them power. He praised their discipline, which he considered vastly superior to that of his own soldiers, and declared, "My countrymen have turned their backs on me and have hated me, because I imposed tribute on them, and sought to bring them under military discipline. You have prevailed against me by means of people brought into a state of discipline."

Then, returning to his defeat, he looked at the predicament then facing him, and, revealing his determination never to surrender, proudly continued:

> Believing myself to be a great lord, I gave you [the British] battle; but, by reason of the worthlessness of my artillery, all my pains were as naught.

> The people of my country, by taunting me with having embraced the religion of the Franks [i.e., Catholicism], and by saying that I had become a Mussulman, and in ten different ways, had provoked me to anger against them. Out of what of evil I have done against them may God bring good. His will be done. I had intended, if God had so decreed, to conquer the whole world; it was my desire to die if my purpose could not be fulfilled. Since the day of my birth till now no man has dared to lay hands on me. Whenever my soldiers began to waver in battle, it was mine to arise and rally them. Last night the darkness hindered me from doing so.

> You people, who have passed the night in joy, may God do unto you as He has done to me. I had hoped, after subduing all my enemies in Abyssinia, to lead my army against Jerusalem, and expel from it the Turks. A warrior who has dandled strong men in his arms will never suffer himself to be dandled in the arms of others.[ii-22]

On completing the above dictation Theodore sat a long time, in the open air, presumably contemplating the future. He then said a prayer, bowed three times to the ground, drank a little water, and suddenly pulled a pistol from his belt, and put it to his mouth. His attempt at suicide was, however, prevented by his men, who snatched the weapon from his hand. As they did so the pistol went off, slightly grazing his ear.

On regaining his composure, Theodore declared that it was not the will of God for him to die. He thereupon turned to the question of the European captives, in the belief, it appears, that by releasing them he could obtain peace. He immediately called a council on their future with his chiefs, all but one of whom recommended that he should kill the prisoners, and fight on to the last. He rejected this advice, however, and decided instead to release the captives.

On the following day, Easter Sunday, 12 April, Theodore, who had been fasting for the previous three days, sent down a letter to Napier, apologising for the brusqueness of his previous communication, and stating that because of the festival—one of the most important of the Ethiopian Church calendar—he was sending the British a gift of cattle, presumably as a peace offering. Turning, finally, to his need for craftsmen, and to his desire for friendship with the British, he concluded, "You require from me all the Europeans, even to my best friend Waldmeier. Well, be it so. They shall go. But now that we are friends you must not leave me without artisans, as I am a lover of the mechanical arts."

Theodore, looking at the situation in Ethiopian terms, seems to have believed that this letter, reinforced by his release of the prisoners and his gift of cattle, marked the end of hostilities. He was reinforced in this view by his secretary, Ato Samwél, who, when asked by the Emperor whether the cattle had been accepted, bowed respectfully, and replied, "The English Ras says to you, 'I have accepted the present.'"[ii-23]

Theodore, we are told, thereupon "heaved a long sigh of relief," for he assumed that peace had been decided upon. The defeated Ethiopian monarch thereupon released his European prisoners, telling the missionary craftsmen that "now that he was friends with the English...he could get as good workmen as they were." He then "bade them farewell in good spirits, under the belief that peace was established.

Never was a surrender, when once resolved upon," writes Markham, "so freely and unreservedly made. Not a hostage, not a child, not a box was kept back. It was the act of a king, an act without cunning or treachery, however slight soever, to mar its fullness."[ii-24]

Napier, however, had no wish to make peace. As he subsequently explained, in a despatch of 14 April, he considered it "essential" for Britain's "national honour" which Theodore had "so grossly insulted," that there should be no negotiation with him, and that "he should be removed for ever from his place."[ii-25] He had therefore at first agreed to accept Theodore's gift; but seeing the number of cattle sent down to his camp, realised that they were intended as a peace-offering, and ordered his men not to receive them.

INTRODUCTION: CAUSES AND CONSEQUENCES

When Theodore, later that evening, learnt that his gift had been rejected, he probably felt that he had been "deceived," as Markham assumes, and realised that a final British assault was imminent.

Understanding the impossibility of his position, the defeated Emperor contemplated flight, on Easter Monday, 13 April; but, finding most of his men reluctant to accompany him, he dismissed them, telling all those not willing to share his fortunes to the end to provide for their own safety. Virtually the whole army then disbanded, only a few chiefs and Theodore's personal followers deciding to remain with him.

The British Commander-in-Chief at about this time decided to "cannonade" Magdala with "all the artillery" at his disposal. That done, a British storming party, firing continuously with their Snider rifles, began the assault on the citadel, at 4 p.m. A quarter of an hour later this party had broken into the fortress, at the gateway of which it found only four dead bodies. The advancing troops then rushed in, and waved the Union Jack in triumph: Magdala had fallen! [ii-26]

Theodore himself fought on for a short time, but almost immediately afterwards dismissed his surviving followers. "Flee," he said, "I release you from your allegiance; as for me, I shall never fall into the hands of the enemy."

As soon as his men had gone, he turned to his sole companion, his faithful valet Walda Gaber, and declared, "It is finished! Sooner than fall into their hands, I will kill myself." He then put a pistol to his mouth, fired the weapon, and fell down dead, thus gaining a unique, and much revered, position in Ethiopian history and mythology. [ii-27]

The victorious British and Indian troops, on finding the body, Markham says, "gave three cheers over it, as if it had been that of a dead fox." [ii-28] They then dispersed to loot the citadel. Within an hour they had succeeded in acquiring a vast amount of manuscripts, many of them beautifully illustrated, as well as processional and crosses, and sundry other booty. [ii-29] Fifteen elephants and almost 200 mules were required to transport it to the coast.

THE END OF THE EXPEDITION

Theodore's death, which, as evident in Simpson's diary, was naturally a source of great rejoicing among the British troops, marked the end of the Magdala Expedition.

On 15 April, only two days after the battle, Napier gave orders for the British troops to prepare for the long journey back to the coast. At that time Britain had no interest whatsoever in Ethiopia, or desire to colonise it. The British government had become involved in matters Ethiopian only on account of Theodore's detention of the European captives, and had moreover promised to withdraw as soon as the latter's liberation had been effected. It was only on that undertaking that the Egyptians had allowed the British to land at the coast, and Dajazmach Kasa to pass through the province of Tegray.

Before leaving Magdala the victorious army destroyed almost all Theodore's artillery, and burnt the citadel to the ground. At the request of his mother, the victors took the Emperor's son and heir, Prince Alamayou, to Britain, where he was befriended by Queen Victoria. He died there without ever returning to his native land.

The Expedition's return journey from Magdala to the coast proved almost as difficult as the original advance. No armed resistance was encountered at any point, but the rainy season had begun, and there were many violent tropical storms which rendered such roads as existed often impassable. Arrived at the port, the troops with the surviving livestock were expeditiously shipped home, where the victors received a rapturous welcome.

In the aftermath of the Emperor's defeat and death, Ethiopia was left still weak and territorially divided. A period of further civil war followed, in which the important nobles struggled for supreme power.

Only when that struggle was resolved could Theodore's successors begin to face the problems with which he had grappled so heroically, but unsuccessfully.

THE PERSONALITY AND HISTORICAL IMPORTANCE OF THEODORE

A final word should be said about the remarkable and complex character of Theodore, which had a significant bearing on his dispute with the British government, and subsequently with the Napier Expedition.

Though Theodore's personality will doubtless long be a matter of debate, there can be no denying that it evoked no little contemporary admiration. The British consul Walter Plowden, who witnessed the Emperor's rise to power, expressed, as we have seen, considerable approval for the Ethiopian ruler. Other foreign observers were also impressed. Yohannes Kotziga, a prominent Greek merchant in the Sudan, who had commercial dealings with Theodore, later described him enthusiastically as "a bold and indefatigable man" with "an extraordinary kind and noble soul." [ii-30] The Swiss missionary Waldmeier, who was at times in close contact with the monarch, spoke of him as a leader who "wanted to civilise his country" and as a kind man. As evidence of this, he recalls an occasion when Theodore, encountering a poor, starving woman in rags, descended from his mule and gave her his own *shamma*, or cotton wrap. [ii-31]

Despite their government's conflict with Theodore, several British observers were scarcely less appreciative. Dufton recalled that he and other European travellers had been "well treated" by the monarch, and remarked, "considering that he could have no other motive for treating us thus but pure kindness, we are bound to testify so far in his favour." Expressing himself forcefully at the very height of the British government's dispute with Theodore, he declared that Theodore was "the first and only patriot Abyssinia ever saw;" and rebutting popular anger against the Emperor in Britain, concluded, "No. Theodore is not all devil! else how comes it that those who have known him best and longest have given the most favourable account of him. Take Bell, for instance, who was his bosom companion, and Plowden, his friend, who both lost their lives in his service." [ii-32]

The British envoy Hormuzd Rassam, who conducted most of the interminable negotiations with the Emperor, and was one of the Magdala captives, was likewise far less critical of the Ethiopian ruler than might be imagined.

Reflecting on the latter's reign, he observed that "notwithstanding all the brutalities practiced by Theodore, he was far more lenient in his judgements than the Fetteh-Negûst [i.e., the traditional Ethiopian legal code] or the common law of Abyssinia....he was not guilty of half the barbarities of Dajjâz [Dajazmach] Oobe [i.e., the ruler of Samen and Tegray] or Sehela Selassê, the Old King of Shoa." Looking at the overall condition of the country during this period, Rassam concluded, "Prior to Theodore's reign, men were deprived of their eyes, tongues, hands, and other members...whereas I believe a traveller might go through the length and breadth of the country without finding a single instance of such mutilation caused by Theodore."[ii-33]

Captain Tristam Speedy, a British officer who had visited Theodore some years earlier, and who served as an interpreter for the Napier Expedition, was scarcely less favourable to the Ethiopian monarch. Speaking after the latter's death, he declared that Theodore was "a man of great ability, brave, generous, and true to his word, with a strange mixture of inordinate pride—and deep humility, extreme gentleness and extreme ferocity."[ii-34]

Clements Markham, one of the Expedition's most perceptive historians, took a not dissimilar view. Likening Theodore to Peter the Great of Russia, he observed, "They were both born kings of men; both endowed with military genius; both lovers of the mechanical arts; both possessed of dauntless courage, and, while capable of noble and generous acts, both were frequently guilty of perpetuating most horrible atrocities."[ii-35]

Such qualified—though generally favourable—comment on Theodore has largely been forgotten by more recent foreign writers, several of whom have chosen to remember only his dark side. Theodore's imprisonment of his European captives, and their long period in detention, caused the popular twentieth century author Alan Moorehead to arrest his readers with the observation that "It has always been accepted that the Emperor Theodore was a mad dog let loose, a sort of reincarnation of Ivan the Terrible and the Russian tyrants, and so he was in many ways, even by the savage standards of Ethiopia itself."[ii-36]

Modern historians of Ethiopia have found it difficult to grapple with Theodore the man, as opposed to Theodore the myth. The Swedish historian

Sven Rubenson, the leading authority on the monarch, has observed that in Theodore,

> Ethiopia received a ruler of a kind very different from any that she had known for many years or even generations, [for] in more than one sense of the word he was a revolutionary...in more than one field of the life of his nation...an innovator of no mean proportions...the first in the line of Emperors to create modern Ethiopia.[ii-37]

Turning to Theodore's character, Rubenson found it "full of contradictions: mysticism and rationalism, consideration and cruelty, humility and pride." Considering the development of Theodore's personality towards the end of his life (in effect, the time of William Simpson's travels to Ethiopia) Rubenson concludes,

> As his feeling of disappointment and frustration grew, his pride and arrogance also seem to have increased, until they bordered on megalomania. He was in so many ways superior to his environment that he could not bear opposition or failure. His actions become less and less predictable or rational. Whether he was at all times fully accountable for what he said and did is at least very doubtful. As former friends and followers deserted him, he must have become an increasingly lonely man, tossed between despair and the forlorn hope of redeeming it all. No one will ever know what his real intentions were when he went to Meqdela [sic]...."[ii-38]

Another modern historian of Ethiopia, the North American Donald Crummey, has also attempted to fathom the complexity of Theodore's character. He considered him "one of the most violent" of all Ethiopian monarchs, "perhaps the most violent," but thought that one had to take account of his "generosity, compassion, and identification with the poor" as well as his "high political objectives: national renewal, modernization, reform, and his concern for Christian morality." Theodore, he believes, nevertheless had a "fatal flaw" in his character: "a kind of pride and overbearing personality which made him impatient of subordinates, a suspicion which made him distrustful of them, and confidence in his own might which led him to an instinctive recourse to violence."[ii-39]

Be all that as it may, there can be no denying the importance of Theodore in Ethiopian—and African—history. It was he who, in the words of the modern Ethiopian historian Bahru Zedwe, "inaugurated [his country's] Modern history."[ii-40] Theodore's reign was at one level a failure but at another a triumph, for it served to chart the future. The Ethiopian monarchs who followed Theodore could scarcely take a single modernising step without treading the road he had trodden, or tried to tread.

Theodore's patriotism, earlier noted by Henry Dufton, and his quest for modernisation, which led him into his fatal conflict with the British, gave him a unique position in the history and mythology of his country. His suicide, which was in a sense the supreme recognition of his failure, won him a permanent place in the hearts and minds of future generations of Ethiopians.

The leading Ethiopian poet, Tsegaye Gabre-Medhin, has written a contemporary play about Theodore which has become a classic.[ii-41] It commemorates the Ethiopian monarch as larger than life. Tsegaye Gabre-Medhin later called on his compatriots to "cherish his memory to the end." [ii-42]

INTRODUCTION:

WILLIAM SIMPSON
ARTIST, ANTIQUARIAN, ETHNOGRAPHER, AND WRITER (1823–1899)

by Peter Harrington

In March 1868 the noted special artist of the *Illustrated London News,* William Simpson, wrote a letter to General Sir Thomas Biddulph, private secretary to Queen Victoria. It read:

> Dear Sir
>
> I have just accepted a commission from the "Illustrated London News" to proceed to Abyssinia for the purpose of illustrating the War. H.S.H. Prince Edward of Saxe Weimar has suggested to me that I ought not to leave without first asking you to inform the Queen of my movements. From the great interest Her Majesty took in my doings in the Crimea, and from the very kind feeling manifested towards me at that time, I think that I may be justified in putting that request to you.
>
> Prince Edward has given me letters of introduction, and I have letters to Sir Robert Napier, which I believe will do all that I require to facilitate the objects I have in view. I have just heard that there are very stringent orders against any one landing at Annesley Bay who is not attached to the Forces, but this difficulty I have no doubt will be easily surmounted.
>
> I remain yours very truly
> William Simpson [iii-1]

Simpson travelled to Abyssinia on behalf of the *ILN* to record in pictures the British military campaign against the Emperor Theodore. For the next few months he would brave the perils of life in a very inhospitable environment;

26

however he was accustomed to the rigors of campaigning with the British Army. He had spent over a year in the Crimea in 1854–55 and observing and sketching the war against Russia.

That William Simpson was writing to the Queen of England illustrates how far he had come since his early days of abject poverty in Scotland. While his career as a special artist has been well documented, his early life is little known.[iii-2] In order to understand the complex man who went on to become one of the leading illustrators of his time, as well as a distinguished archaeologist and ethnographer, it is important to understand his early years and the various events and influences that shaped him.

CHILDHOOD AND APPRENTICESHIP

Simpson was born in Glasgow on 28 October 1823 and spent the first two decades of his life moving around from place to place, due to his father's frequent job changes. James Simpson was a clever man and an engineer by trade; however he failed to apply himself to his work, preferring instead to spend his spare time drinking with his friends. More often than not, he would return home inebriated, and his frequent outbursts of violence toward his wife were the cause of great anxiety for the young boy. It was a constant struggle for William's mother to make ends meet for her husband and only child.

In later life it pained him to write about his unfortunate childhood and the 'wretched condition' of his family life. The principal source of information is a manuscript entitled "Notes and recollections of my life" which was written down for the information of his young daughter. This is now in the National Library of Scotland in Edinburgh. It was used as the basis of his published *Autobiography* but many painful observations—especially about his father's conduct—were omitted.[iii-3]

The boy was sent to live with his grandmother in Perth for a short period in 1834–35, to assist her and provide companionship. His only formal schooling took place during this time, when his grandmother sent him to what she considered to be the finest writing school in Scotland. His family wanted him to become an engineer, so once back in Glasgow he was apprenticed to the firm of Macfarlane, working in their small lithographic office.

Simpson said later that "this was the turning point which changed all my boyish intentions." He developed skills in all forms of lithography. He also attended the free introductory lectures in the arts and sciences at the nearby Andersonian University and the Mechanics Institute. Impressed with the progress of his young apprentice, Mr. Macfarlane enrolled him in a series of lectures on natural philosophy at the Gorbals Popular Institution. In the winter of 1838–39 Simpson took the architectural and mechanical drawing class at the Andersonian and won first prize for a mechanical drawing of a steam engine.

Simpson described himself at this time as

> Patient, industrious, and working hard to improve myself in any way I could, and it brought me often into circumstances which contrasted widely with the miserable conditions of the home in which I had to live. Generally I was wretchedly clad, all but a ragged boy, often with no shoes or stockings, as boys in Scotland often are, yet I was ready whenever I could get the chance, studying Philosophy and Chemistry, learning Architecture, and taking a prize. How often I longed in those days, when I was beginning to grow up, that I had better clothes, so that I could have a more respectable appearance. ("Notes," 23)

He left Macfarlane's shortly after and spent six months in a muslin warehouse where he was given the opportunity of designing and lithographing fabric patterns. The increase in pay was welcome, as his father was out of work again. Simpson was turning increasingly towards art and away from engineering; his time at the warehouse was short-lived and he went in search of a position with a lithographic company. He succeeded in finding suitable employment with Allan and Ferguson. For the next few years he worked to hone his skills as an apprentice, while his home life continued to be miserable; "it was my mother's devotion that kept us alive," he wrote.

At his new workplace he began to draw directly on stone for the first time, and his efforts brought him to the attention of Mr. Allan, who had him make

28

a series of designs for houses, churches and public buildings. "The first plate I did was so satisfactory, that when Mr. Allan had a proof brought to him by the printer, he came in with it in his hand and complimented me upon it." ("Notes," 25)

The office closed early on Saturdays and this allowed Simpson to head out to the country to sketch. He was forced to stay home on Sundays because "I had no clothes to appear in on Sunday, so I seldom went out on that day, but generally practised in the house. When things improved later I was able to get out to the country and sketch on that day also."("Notes," 26)

His sketching was restricted to pencil work as he could not afford water colours until he hit upon an idea:

> On days that my mother was out working, no dinner could be made in the house and a penny was allotted for me to supply myself—a very small sum,—but by taking a walk in the dinner hour, which I generally did by Queen Street and Buchanan Street, where I could see pictures, water colour drawings in the Carver and Gilder's shop windows, I saved my penny, and was able to buy colours in the colour shops....a penny worth of ochre, for instance, would make nearly a dozen cakes of colour and the same with a good many others. ("Notes," 26)

The more he practiced the better he became, and he started to make a little extra money doing portraits of friends. His mother would invite people to her house to have their portraits taken by "Willie." He was attending evening classes in art at the School of Design and progressing at work to the extent that Mr. Allan began to notice his creative efforts and gave the young man money to visit Edinburgh to see the exhibition at the Royal Scottish Academy. Simpson later wrote, "I have always felt that Mr. Allan was more of a father to me than my own." His situation at home was getting worse and his family had sunk into deep poverty. His father had been unemployed for three years; the drinking continued, and on more than one occasion William had to intervene to restrain his father from striking his mother. He threatened to leave the house if his father did not change his ways, but stayed on to protect his mother.

Allan and Ferguson began to benefit from the numerous railway schemes that were being proposed in the 1840s, and Simpson was responsible for lithographing many of the plans. He received a bonus for all the extra hours he put in and the additional money made life easier. As a little boy he had told his mother that one day he would buy her a silk dress; the day came in 1845 that he was able to fulfill this desire: "It was one of the highest pleasures to me to do it, and it was to her the same on putting it on." His increased wages also allowed him to purchase better clothes for himself, especially a Sunday suit.

Simpson started making sketches that were to be lithographed.

> This also gave me a better class of work—what was called 'chalk'—the name given to lithographic crayons, [it] was the higher branch of a litho-graphic draughtsman's department, and I came now into this class of work. ("Notes," 29)

He prepared sketches of the River Clyde and the Scottish highlands, which he made into lithographs for sale by the company. He also used old houses of Glasgow as the subject of lithographs, and they were published in *Views and Notices of Glasgow in Former Times* (although Simpson's name did not appear in the book.)

His fascination with archaeology seems to have started from these old buildings in Glasgow:

> [It] awakened in me the archaeological instinct of my nature. The instinct was already there for I well remember when in Perth...that I was thus attracted to the crumbling stones of these places. I recollect looking at these, and wondering at them as witnesses of time. It was [from] the old houses of Glasgow, and the sketching of them that I developed this feeling, and led me to become an Archaeologist (Ibid).

He was now an avid reader of everything from theology to geology, at a time when evolutionary ideas were at odds with religious teaching. He moved on to French grammar and to poetry, developing a passion for Scottish songs, English poetry and the works of Keats, and devoured books on literary criticism. He joined a society of young artists in Glasgow and its small library was a revelation for him. His mind was opened to art history by Joshua Reynolds' *Discourses* and *Modern Painters* by the young 'graduate of Oxford,' John Ruskin.

He exhibited his first picture, called "Garscadden Gates," at the annual exhibition of the West of Scotland Academy towards the end of the 1840s, and in 1850 sold his picture "The Braes of Lochaber."

FROM GLASGOW TO LONDON

1851 was a turning point in William Simpson's career. Having served four years with Allan and Ferguson, the then twenty-seven year old journeyed to London (on the advice of Mr. Allan), to progress as an artist. He set off in search of work in the metropolis on the first Tuesday of February; "I knew that Day and Son's place was the principal one in London, more particularly for Artistic work, so I settled to apply there first." He was hired immediately as a lithographer, starting at £2 a week; his salary was soon raised to £6 and ultimately to £8.

The style of work at Day's was far superior to what he was accustomed to in Glasgow. "It was to this superior standard I had to work myself up to, but thanks to constant practice in Glasgow, to painting in the morning, School of Design at night, and constant sketching out of doors from nature, I was not long in establishing my position in the new field of action." He described himself as "perhaps the most useful artist in the place." Many architectural subjects—such as new churches and public buildings—passed through his hands, in addition to scenes of public events and portraits of singers, dancers, actors, and Members of Parliament.

He saw important works of art such as David Robert's "Destruction of Jerusalem," James Atkinson's "Afghanistan," and several series of lithographs depicting wars in India and South Africa. Lithography had at this time reached its zenith as the form of choice for reproductions; but within twenty years it would be completely eclipsed by the cheaper process of wood engraving, and indeed virtually all of Simpson's professional work for the illustrated press was in the form of wood engravings. Simpson was kept so busy drafting scenes of the Great Exhibition, which were in great demand, that it was not for several months that he was able to see the Exhibition for himself. In September 1851 he brought his parents down from Scotland to live with him in the North London suburb of Kentish Town.

His mother died there on August 24, 1854. He described her later as

> One of the best of mothers. I owe everything to her, and it was a great satisfaction to me that I was able to make the last few years of her life comfortable and happy. My success so far, was of course a source of happiness to her also, and I always felt a deep regret that she did not live a few years longer, to have had the further pleasure of enjoying the still greater success which fell to my lot, from the work I produced in the Crimean War. ("Notes," 38)

PROFESSIONAL MATURITY

Simpson's subsequent career is well documented. The following summary will place his work in Abyssinia into context.

Simpson was sent to the Crimea in 1854 by the London publishing firm of Colnaghi, to create images suitable for lithographing. He spent several months producing sketches and watercolours of the battles and scenes there. (During this period he also accompanied the Duke of Newcastle on an expedition to Circassia where he had the opportunity to study the native population, with its diverse customs and traditions.)[iii-4] The watercolours were sent back to England and redrawn onto lithographic plates, then sold in sets of 80 prints titled *The Seat of War in the East,* which were very popular.[iii-5] This publication brought him immediate fame:

> Among my friends my common name was "Crimean Simpson" and as a Crimean Hero I was introduced to strangers as, "Mr. Simpson from the Crimea," but Crimean Heroes became so common after the war, that one day I was introduced to a gentleman with the usual formula that I was from the Crimea, and he said, "Well, I am Mr. Smith who has not been to the Crimea," and he had, I must confess, the best of it, so far as celebrity was concerned. ("Notes," 55)

Queen Victoria herself developed a strong interest in his work and complimented the artist for being under fire. "The Queen was so easy and natural in her manner that I was not at any moment of the interview in the least embarrassment, but stood speaking to her as if she had been any lady I had had to talk to." His frequent visits to Buckingham Palace and Windsor brought him into contact with other members of the Royal family and he became acquainted with the Prince of Wales, the Princess Royal, and the Empress of Germany. Throughout the rest of his life he attended numerous royal events, and he received many commissions for portraits and sketches from the royal family.

The success of the Crimean venture provided the impetus for a similar project for Day and Sons, illustrating the rebellion in India which had concluded in 1858. Simpson's sojourn in the Indian sub-continent resulted in over 250 pictures depicting landscapes, palaces and other buildings, portraits, and scenes.[iii-6] Unfortunately while he was travelling around India his employers went into bankruptcy. The fifty pictures that had been made into lithographs were wed with a text hastily written by Sir John Kaye and published as a large folio volume, *India Ancient and Modern.*

Simpson had done occasional freelance work for the *Illustrated London News* in the late 1850s.[iii-7] The paper needed special artists on the spot; they had been caught unprepared at the beginning of the Crimean war and it was several months before their artists reached the scene of the fighting. Aware of Simpson's talent for producing rapid but accurate sketches, they approached him with an offer to send him to St. Petersburg in 1866 to record the marriage of the Czarevitch to Princess Dagmar. This was the start of Simpson's close association with the *ILN,* which lasted over thirty years.

Two years later the *ILN* sent Simpson to Abyssinia. In addition to covering the military operations, Simpson was increasingly drawn to the antiquities in Abyssinia as well as the customs and traditions of its people, and he extensively recorded what he observed. His later papers on these observations were among the first of many scholarly reports from his hand, which demonstrated a clear understanding of architectural and archaeological concepts. His numerous scholarly papers are a testimony to his thorough understanding of ancient cultures.[iii-8]

Upon his return to London, Simpson once again wrote to Sir Thomas Biddulph at Windsor:

> Dear Sir
>
> Your letter of March last followed me to Abyssinia, where I received it with its kind message from Her Majesty.
>
> Since then I have returned, and have now made a number of my sketches into pictures. And I write to ask if Her Majesty desires to see them. Those that I have already finished are pictures of Magdala, and one or two drawings of the ceremonies of the Abyssinian Church, and a drawing of the rock-cut Church at Dongolo, which is one of the oldest Christian churches in the world.
>
> I may say that it would add to the interest of the drawings were I to attend and explain them, but in this I will act only according to your instructions.
>
> > Believe me
> > Yours truly
> > William Simpson[iii-9]

Biddulph sent a note to Queen Victoria to which Her Majesty added, "Let him bring them some day next week at 1/2 2."[iii-10] Simpson visited Windsor on Friday, 20 November and left his portfolio for the Queen to examine. He wrote on the 30th:

> Sir Thomas Biddulph promised to telegraph to me in the beginning of the week after I was at Windsor, but as yet I have not received an order to come again to submit and explain my drawings. As I fear that such a trifling matter may have been forgotten, I merely drop this note to ask you if you would oblige by reminding Sir Thomas of the matter. I left the portfolio, and one of the drawings is a commission, and I ought to send [it] to Florence without delay. So I will take it as a kindness if you recall to their memory the promise that was made.[iii-11]

Simpson was by now quite the celebrity and was frequently in the company of royalty or the aristocracy as well as academics. He presented papers to learned societies—on subjects ranging from Buddhist prayer wheels and the origin of the Prince of Wales' feathers, to the archaeology of Jerusalem, Mycenae, Ephesus, and Troy. (He had visited the site of Troy during Schlieman's excavations in 1877.)

The 1870s were a busy decade for Simpson. He went to France to cover the war between Napoleon III and Prussia, which was soon followed by the revolution in Paris known as the Commune. It was during the Franco-Prussian war that Simpson was arrested on suspicion of spying, but quickly released.[iii-12] A journey in 1872 took him around the world for the *ILN*, covering various events and subjects which included the marriage of the Emperor of China. On his return from the Far East he covered the fighting in the Lava Beds of northern California between the United States Army and the Modoc Indians. His book *Meeting the Sun: A Journey Round the World* was published in 1873, with much of the text based on his letters to the *Daily News*. He continued writing for the *Daily News* during the Afghanistan war in 1878, in addition to sending many sketches to the *ILN*.

Simpson visited South Asia on several occasions, the most recent being his trip to India in 1877 to accompany the Prince of Wales, and he was well acquainted with the Indian sub-continent. When he visited Afghanistan he took advantage of the opportunity to explore the ancient Buddhist remains there, including the excavation of an ancient Buddhist tope using soldiers supplied by the army. His explorations resulted in several presentations to London societies and publication of various papers.

In 1879, while in Bombay on his return from Afghanistan, he received news that his father had died in Glasgow at the age of 88. He wrote, "Passed a very quiet afternoon in my room. Strange thoughts, thinking on the news of the morning."[iii-13]

In 1881 he married Marie Eliza Burt, 18 years his junior, and bought a large house in Willesdon, north London. (Simpson was 58, his wife being 40 in that year.) He had probably known her for the previous 15 years, but his work had kept him away from Britain. She was an accomplished painter of miniatures who had exhibited at the Royal Academy. Their only child, Ann Penelope, was born on 28 January, 1884.

A few years later he was back in Afghanistan, this time accompanying the Afghan Boundary Commission, which was to delineate the northern boundary of the country where it bordered Russia. This was to be his last major overseas tour as his health had begun to suffer; he had frequent bouts of fever, probably as a result of malaria.

His final working years were spent covering events at home and on the Continent, and he continued to write and lecture on subjects from far afield based on his personal observations from prior visits. He was active with the Palestine Exploration Fund, the Society for Biblical Archaeology, and the Royal Asiatic Society. His papers appeared frequently in the journals of these groups. He participated in the exhibitions of the Royal Institute of Painters in Water-Colour and became a member of that group, which enabled him to put the initials "R.I." after his name, along with the initials of the Royal Institute of British Architects and the Royal Geographical Society.

Simpson continued his regular visits to the Queen at Windsor, Balmoral and Sandringham. He was summoned on behalf of the Royal family to sketch the Duke of Albany and later the Duke of Clarence on their deathbeds. The Prince of Wales called him his "dear old friend."

His editor approached him in 1893 about going to cover the Great Exhibition in Chicago, but his doctors advised against it:

> I am now close on the end of my 70th year, and for the last 39 years, I have been a sort of Wandering Jew, but now at last I begin to feel the effects of age. After so many years spent in this way, it is not without a feeling of regret I at last realize that at least one part of my career has come to an end. ("Notes," 241)

According to George Eyre-Todd, who edited Simpson's memoirs for publication in 1903, the aging artist caught a chill in 1890 at the opening of the Forth Bridge (near Edinburgh) by the Prince of Wales. This led to bronchitis, which "laid him aside, more or less, during these last years and proved fatal in the end." He died at Willesdon on August 17, 1899, his wife and daughter at his side. He was buried in Highgate Cemetery next to his mother; his headstone bore the title, "The Pioneer of War Artists."

A memorial exhibition of his sketches was held at the Henry Graves gallery in Pall Mall in 1900. The exhibition catalogue summed up his career:

> The works of this extraordinary man, whose name is a household word in many parts of the world, show wonderful drawing exquisite colour, and the most careful attention to detail, and his tireless energy and indefatigable labour, combined with the excellence of his work, whether executed under conditions of temperature below zero, malarial climes, or the fire of an enemy, afloat, or ashore, can only be the subject of admiration and wonder to those who knew him personally, or by his works.[iii-14]

Diary of a Journey to Abyssinia

The Diary and Observations

of

William Simpson

THE SONG OF THE ABYSSINIAN CAPTIVES

Oh weary the hours, and dreary the days,
And night only comes to deepen the woe;
Our souls must struggle with doubts and delays;
Our bodies with chains are gall'd by our foe.
Our tears, our tears, they have fallen unseen,
And our griefs by our groans have been told;
For years, long years, our bondage has been,
Till no more can the bitter cup hold.

Though it is a land both pleasant and fair,
And with flesh pots like the Egypt of yore,
Yet he that hath breathed of freedom's pure air,
Still must be thinking to breathe it once more.
Our bondage seems as the darkness of sin,
Like Israel's children we would go in peace,
But Pharaoh's heart it is hardened within;
The Strong Arm alone can bring our release.

At last the Strong Arm we hear that it comes;
By rumour each day we learn it draws near;
And while we hope for our freedom and homes,
It is the despot's fierce passion we fear.
Let them come! Let them come! Brave men in ranks.
– Oh, let them come! Death or life let it be!
If it is life, then let to God be the thanks;
If it is death, still, then still we are Free!

William Simpson
Red Sea, March 1868

40

†HE OU†WARD jOURNEY

PART I: **London to Annesley Bay**
3 March to 25 March 1868

3 March, Tue. Left London per S. Chatham-Dover Rail. Ludgate Hill Station at 8.30 p.m. Had a fine quick passage to Calais, and arrived in Paris at 7.30 a.m.

4 March, Wed. Got my baggage to a hotel at the Lyons Railway Station. Had breakfast and then called upon A. H. at 22 Rue de l'Arcade, who accompanied me to do a little sight seeing. We passed the site of the Great Exhibition of '67, and saw a little of the building. We afterwards visited the Cathedral of Notre Dame, La Sainte Chapelle, the Hotel Cluny, and I was much struck with the old part of it, said to be as old as the time of Caesar. I was much struck with its high, circular, arched roof, showing that *stone roofs* are not a new idea, nor so peculiar as Marcus Keane seems to think.[1-1]

5 March, Thur. I met Annie by appointment at the Louvre where we spent the forenoon. It rained in the afternoon, so we had to confine our movements to the Arcades of the Palais Royal. Towards six o'clock it cleared up, and we had a stroll very near[ly] as far as the Arc de Triomphe. I returned to the Lyons Railway Station and left at 10.45 [p.m.] for Marseille.[1-2]

6 March, Fri. All day in the Railway. Had some breakfast at Dijon. Dinner at Lyons, where I met a gentleman who turned out to be an artist, and acquaint[ed] with the Hay family in Scotland. He gave me his name: Mr. Cyrus Macrire, 30 Rue d'Hautville, Paris; and I promised to call on my return. I was very ill afterwards, which I attributed to the wine.

7 March, Sat. At 4.30 a.m. I arrived at Marseille and was taken by the Coches [stage coaches] to the Hotel de la Méditerranée, Place St. Louis, where I went to bed and slept till about nine o'clock. Still bad in the bowels. Called at the P.T.O. office [Post and Telegraph Office] and found a letter from my coz. [cousin] with two enclosures, one from Mr. Allen, and the other from the Rev. W. D. Parish with a letter of introduction to his Brother commanding the 45th Regiment in Abyssinia.[1-3] I then walked about the town and was struck with the changes since '54 and '55. I went to the Chapel of Notre Dame de la Garde and found an entire new erection, in Byzantine architecture. I had a chat on the way up with an old woman selling charms, pictures, crosses. Our conversation got upon the Virgin, who, she declared, was my mother, her mother, and the mother of all who are born, and that when we have her we need no other Father or Mother. This I quite admired for it was a complete doctrine of the east, and was a most emphatic declaration that Mary is the Sancti of the Jehovistic Lingo. I returned to the hotel and had dinner, and then went aboard the *Pera* with my luggage. Slept on board.

8 March, Sun. Left Marseille at 10 a.m. A beautiful day and a fair wind. Passed quite close to the Chateau d'If.

9 March, Mon. Before I got on deck we had passed the straits between Sardinia and Corsica. I could still see on the Starboard the high hills of Sardinia.

10 March, Tue. About six in the morning we passed Stromboli, and the Lipari (or Eolian) islands, and had a fine view of Aetna. After breakfast we entered the straits of Messina, and had a fine sail through them. Aetna is not visible while passing through but it appeared again as we cleared the southern end.

11 March, Wed. Nothing particular to notice, scarcely a sail to be seen. An Alexandria Pilot, Haji Mahomed, on board told me that the "Harám" at the Caaba was with the left shoulder to the pivot; he did not use that mode of expression, but used it as the least unmistakable term by which to describe the mode of circumambulating the shrine at Mecca, which Haji Mahomed said was three times, washing and drinking the water of Zem-Zem.[1-4]

12 March, Thur. Same as yesterday, passed one vessel and signalled.

13 March, Fri. Arrived at Alexandria at 10 a.m. Bailey came with me in the boat, and we passed the Custom House, which was a great trial of patience.

Simpson recalls:

As I was not going to India, my luggage had to pass through the Custom House, which was a troublesome affair. I shall never forget one man looking down the barrel of my revolver. (*Autobiography*, 184)

We then got "the only two honest men in Alexandria" who carried my luggage through the street to the Hotel. Got two donkeys and started for Pompey's pillar, and returned by Cleopatra's Needle. Had tiffin [lunch, snack] in the Hotel with Cursetjee, the Bombay judge,[1-5] and then got to the Station in time to catch the train at 3.10 p.m. Reached Cairo at 9 p.m. Went to the new Oriental Hotel.

14 March, Sat. Got up at 6 a.m. and started with Bailey, and [an]other two of our passengers in a carriage for the Grand Mosque and had a fine view of Cairo, including the pyramids. Left Cairo at 10 A.M., and reached Suez about 5 p.m.[1-6] Met Captain Arbuthnot*[1-7] bound for Abyssinia and through him I learned that a steamer would sail on Monday direct to Annesley Bay, and [he] advised me to arrange to go with it. Major Stansfeld* is the man who is in charge here, and would no doubt give me a passage. Met Mr. Pritchard in the Hotel en route for England from Calcutta. French concert at night.

15 March, Sun. Saw Major Stansfeld who promised me a passage, but told me how strict his orders were on this point.

Elaborating on the difficulty of obtaining the passage, Simpson later observed:

Major Stansfeld was in charge at Suez, so I applied to him for a passage. He was particular as to my credentials, so I showed him a letter of introduction to Sir Robert Napier,* which I think had the Duke of Cambridge's name or initials on the envelope. This satisfied him and he made an apologetic explanation. He said many had come making a request to go to Zoulla,[1-8] and only the other day one man had applied, stating that he had a letter from Sir Stafford Northcote, who was Secretary of State for India at the time. Major Stansfeld luckily had asked to see the letter, and it turned out to be a note from Sir Stafford refusing to recommend him. With this bit of experience it was necessary to be careful. (*Autobiography*, 185–186)

Captain Arbuthnot kindly sent through to Cairo for a horse for me.

16 March, Mon. I have been a good deal about the bazaar. Made the acquaintance of some Smyrna Jews. One told me he was a Protestant, and another that he only believed in one great God. He had left his wife at Smyrna, and had another in Suez. It cost him 10 francs a day to live. They had all photographs of a very immoral kind for sale, and one of them produced a box full of "French letters" [condoms] which he sold. I told them they were very bad Jews. Found 5 Crim[ean] Tartars in the bazaar on their way to Mecca, also met two Circassians from Dagistan. I mentioned Shumyl's name to them, and they looked pleased at hearing it.

> [Simpson here copies a bill for 10/ [10 shillings] for shipping his horse on the *Koina*]

This was for my Horse which I named "Cheops." I also took a small Donkey off Arbuthnot's hands, which he had no need for, and christened him "Teodorus"—Theodore, in honour of the Emperor of Abyssinia.

I also met a man from Khorassar and another from Bokhara, all en route for Mecca. I bought a few articles, and in the afternoon I went off again in the *penguin* [local water taxi] with Luckhart,* with my luggage, to board the *Koina*[1-9] bound for Annesley Bay. We were to take a transport laden with camels. The name of the transport was *Sam Cearns.*[1-10] Arbuthnot came on board about 6 o'clock, and it was some time after dark as we started. We had a difficulty in making a start with the ship in tow. She would not start at first.

17 March, Tue. At seven a.m. this morning we were at the Lighthouse on the west coast, which is about 50 miles from Suez, and were making about 4 miles an hour. The coast on each side is very rugged and barren, with fine picturesque hills.

18 March, Wed. This morning, when I got upon deck about 6 o'clock, we were passing out of the straits of Jubal. The Island of Shadwan was on our Starboard, and in the distance on the other side was the peninsula of Sinai which terminate[s] at Ras Mahomed. At breakfast time we had [our] last sight of these but we saw the peaks of the African coast all day.[1-11]

19 March, Thur. No land visible to-day. We passed the Brothers, two islands, last night.[1-12] We have still a good favourable breeze with us. 130 mile, at 12 to-day, passed a lighthouse standing out of the water. It is on a coral reef. Four Europeans have charge of it, three are always in the light-house, and one away on three months leave. It seemed very solitary. They showed the Turkish flag.

20 March, Friday. Playing quoits with Captain Sampson.

21 March, Sat. No wind today. Sea perfectly calm. Saw a steamer to the westward with a ship in tow, going for Suez. In the afternoon the *Sidees*, or Negroes, who are employed as coal trimmers, were dancing forward.[1-13] Mr. Christie, the Chief Engineer, called me to see them. They muttered some words to a doggerel air and clapped their hands and stamped with their feet on the deck.

22 March, Sun. When I got on deck this morning about 5 o'clock the sun was not up, and the waning moon was not far above the horizon, very bright, and the unilluminated portion of the moon was clearly visible. Slept on one of the sofas in the Saloon on account of the heat, and felt better this morning.

23 March, Mon. A very fine day, but hot. Thermometer above 80.

One of the "shames" [rumours] reported about Sir Robert Napier was that "things had come to a pretty *pass* when he was trying to *pass* through an im*pass*able *pass*."[1-14]

24 March, Tue. Last night finished our week at sea. This morning land in sight on the African coast, and an island on our port bow.

SHOHOS BRINGING IN GRASS TO THE COMMISSARIAT AT UNDEL WELLS

46

PART II: **THE JOURNEY TO ADIGERAT**
26 March - 5 April, 1868
Includes Easter Sunday

25 March, Wed. Zoulla. This morning we got into Annesley Bay [also known as Zoulla or Zoola] at about 3 a.m. (Ghubbet Dacnoo is the native name of Annesley Bay.) All the ships had lights up, which made a very fine sight. The stars were very clear, the Pole Star was visible far down on the horizon and the Southern Cross was visible in the opposite side of the heavens.

In the early morning when the day began to dawn the locality seemed more like a farm yard than the base of war operations. The poultry in the ships began to make sounds and Chanticleer announced the morn in loud sounds from many quarters round. Ducks also expressed their feelings in their own manner, and the grunting of pigs was not one of the least of the sounds.

Went on shore with Arbuthnot and got Sir J. Biddulph's* letter with the Queen's wishes for my success. Called on Commodore Heath* and there found Roberts* and was introduced to General Stewart,* who promised to take me with him.

> I found here an old Balaclava friend, Captain Heath, R.N.[2-1] He was commodore, with his flag flying on board a man-of-war in the bay. I went on board to see him, and met General Donald Stewart, who was starting for Senafe next day, and kindly offered to take me with him if I could be ready. As it would be something to make a start on my long journey to the front under such auspices, I set to work at my arrangements, and managed to do this.
>
> Servants were necessary, and I trusted to find Indians at Zoulla. My Hindustani would enable me to employ them. There was a lot about to sail next day back to India, and they were mustered out for my inspection and selection. A miserable collection they seemed. It occurred to me that if I chanced to select men who had the desire to go home, I might find them unwilling servants; so I said that as it was difficult to choose, I should prefer volunteers. Two turned out of the rank, and the thing was settled. (*Autobiography*, 186–187)

26 March, Thur. Zoulla. I came on shore with my traps and slept in Roberts' tent to be able to leave early in the morning.

> *Simpson describes his brief stop-over at Zoulla, site of the old Aksumite port of Adulis:*

> Some of the [Royal] Engineer Corps uncovered the remains of an old Greek church. Only the foundations were left, but I made a sketch of them. Nothing of the old city was visible above ground."[2-2] (*Autobiography*, 186)

27 March, Friday. Koomaylee. Left Zoulla with the General and Captain Fellowes* and rode on to Koomaylee, said to be 13 miles. Major Nuttall* had breakfast for us.

I made my first march this morning as far as this place [Koomaylee] which is at the foot of the hills and the entrance of the pass. We left at about half-past nine, as the sun was rising among the shipping in Annesley Bay, and the *Shohos* of the neighbourhood were coming in to Zoulla to their work at the commissariat, transport and other departments.[2-3]

At first the way was over a plain deep in dust but soon we reached bushes and slight vegetation, and the latter part of the way was stony as well as dusty. We had not gone far when we heard the sound of a train, which was going out with stores. The railway is in working order for about 9 miles, and it is being completed to Koomaylee and it is promised to be in working order the whole way—thirteen miles, in three weeks.[2-4]

About half way to Koomaylee there is a short range of low hills and at the foot of them Major Chamberlain*[2-5] of the 23rd Pioneers discovered water and dug some wells which supplied the railway, and it was made the station or hospital for sick mules. But the great place for water is Koomaylee, and it is a very important station as the starting point of all transport along the pass.

> A plentiful supply of water has been got at this place by digging wells and pumping it up. Both suction and chain pumps are used. There are three of these, but it does not require them all to supply the water for the

animals. Seven thousand animals could be watered every day, if it were needed. A working party is told off to work the pump, and by changing the men a continuous run of pure clear water is kept up. This is led, by means of wooden troughs, along a considerable space, and the animals are led down by the conductors in companies. They are very difficult to manage, as they get excited at the sound of the water, and rush at it, in their eager desire to drink, producing confusion everywhere.

Sentries are stationed to regulate their turns to drink, and fences are put up to keep them in order and in their turns. In the evening, when they come down to water, it is a most animated scene. The camels, with their long necks stretched out in the direction of the water, become excited, and produce that disagreeable gurgling roar which is so painful to listen to. Great bullocks from Goojerat come on with a steady step; mules and horses tear, pull, and kick; conductors swear in English or abuse in Hindostanee; and the attendants, who have been picked up in all the bazaars of the East, talk and shout in every language that Babel gave birth to. (*ILN*, 9 May 1868)

The station is in charge of Major Nuttall. The Bombay 2nd. Grenadiers are at this point. Although this is the country of the Shohos yet there are Abyssinians [i.e., Christian highlanders] who have come down in numbers to work and pick up what they can. They are very anxious to inform you that they are "Christo," and not Mahomedans, and they also manifest a deep interest regarding the faith of Europeans, and although they know very well yet ask if we also are "Christo," and when answered in the affirmative they say *tayib*, or good.[2-6]

As Abyssinia stands like an island within a sea of Mohammedanism all round it, and as that sea is an enemy always trying to encroach, it was naturally an interesting event to the Abyssinians to see such a novelty as the people of another nation with the same faith as their own. If one stopped to speak to any of the natives on the way, the word "Christian," with an interrogative accent, assisted with the finger pointed at you, was the beginning of conversation, and when they got a satisfactory reply, they expressed themselves generally by the Arabic, tayib, or "good." But the absence of the blue cord round our necks[2-7] often produced great doubts about our religion; they would pull out their own, and then they would with their own hands search among our clothes to find what they considered

as the essential emblem of Christianity. When they could find no such indication they would mutter the words "Moslim?" or "Hindee?" When satisfied that we were neither the one nor the other, they would call out, "Christian, *tayib*," and they would repeat these words till we did the same. In fact, so familiar did this phrase become to us, and so frequent was its repetition on the march, that it became a mode of salutation between us and the Abyssinians.

Simpson elaborates on this cord: "When an Abyssinian is baptized he receives a blue cord, which he wears round his neck....

ALI, A SHOHO OF THE DANAKIL TRIBE

Ultimately I procured one of these blue cords and wore it. This saved me from further trouble with the natives. (*Autobiography*, 190)

28 March, Sat. Sooroo. Started about 1/2 past 5, and rode on to Upper Sooroo, through the Sooroo pass.[2-8] Saw two monkeys shot by a naturalist.

This is the first station up the pass, and is about 12 miles from Koomalyee. It is in the pass that one is first struck with the wonderfully good road which has been made. In some places, or it ought to be said that almost the whole way, instead of having the appearance of a temporary road, made only a week or so ago, [it] bears the aspect of being a perfectly constructed work, kept in good repair, and it carries with it the idea that it must have been there for centuries; no one, if he did not know, would doubt but the road was one of the old institutions of the country, and yet it is in its whole length, of about 50 miles, merely the bed of a mountain torrent, and a few days [of] heavy rain must inevitably transform it back again to this character. The road is very level, and in some places as smooth as the best Macadam or the Kunkur of India, and men are told off to pick up the stones.[2-9]

That part of it called the Sooroo Pass, which is also called the "Devil's Staircase," is one of the wildest passes I have ever seen. It extends over some miles, and has high precipitous rock on each side, with here and there huge blocks filling up the pass which have fallen down. These here have been in some cases blown to pieces by powder, and in others the spaces between have been filled up so as to make a good road. All this must have been a work of great labour, and is most creditable to all employed upon it.[2-10]

Sooroo is a place where there is a little open space, and it is a very little bit of space, where the animals and stores can get room to rest on in their passage to the front. The hills are very rugged and precipitous. All the rock seems in loose masses of debris, with little or no vegetation.

> I had almost 250 miles—that is, in straight line, not counting bends in the road—from Zoulla to Magdala. Myself, horse, donkey, and two villainous-looking servants were the band setting out. I took no tents, as I learned that there were camping-grounds, or stations, at regular intervals along the whole distance, and that tents would be found at each station for travellers passing to and fro.

> One of my early experiences in one of these tents was in the Sooroo Pass. Repeatedly during the night I got up, walked some distance off, divested myself of my sleeping costume, and shook it in the wind, beating it against whatever was to hand. But on my return I was soon as bad as ever. The population of that tent must have been something enormous. However, I managed to derive one satisfaction out of that unhappy night. I caught one of my tormentors, and sent it home to Bonomi. He took it to the British Museum, to the natural history department, and they expressed great satisfaction at receiving it. They told Bonomi that travellers, mighty Nimrods of the chase, brought home and offered the Museum the results of their hunting, which were generally big animals, which the authorities already had, and knew all about, as there were as a rule no varieties of them; but as for the smaller creatures, such as the insect

tribes, of which there are so many varieties, no one thought of sending them. So one of my "back-biters" has been reformed and converted into a teacher of science. (*Autobiography*, 187)

29 March, Sunday. Undel Wells. Came on to this place, pass very wild, bare and rugged.[2-11]

Text accompanying a Simpson drawing of Shohos bringing grass to Undel Wells: (see page 46)

The Commissariat officers on the road are very particular in their endeavours to keep the Shohos at this work of bringing in grass, because it saves the carriage of forage from Zoulla for the pack animals. The result is, that at every station a great number of them work willingly at this useful task of supplying stores. The price given is about a dollar for 100 lb., and a ration of rice is given them. The figures here shown give an idea of the female Shoho, who carries the heaviest loads. Her costume is formed of one piece of leather which covers the body from the bosom to the knees. This skin is generally ornamented with a few cowries. The middle portion of the head is either shaved or very closely cut, and a fringe of hair is left before and behind. These are plaited, and the mass behind looks very like the present fashion of chignons. (*ILN*, published 9 May 1868)

At Undel Wells we saw two Mohammedan girls who were going off from near Goun-Goona with soldiers of the Beloochie Regiment [27th Bombay Native Infantry; or BNI]. The officers at Undel Wells did not know very well how to act in the case. The connection could not be expected to be anything else than a loose one, and yet as they were escaping from a state of something like slavery, it seemed hard to interfere. The girls themselves said that we might kill them but they would not return. They wanted someone to give them food, and they would be faithful servants to any man that would be husbands to them and be their protectors. This was a very common-sense view, and I think that the judgment was to let them proceed.

30 March, Mon. Rayray Guddy. A long march of 18 miles. Some large trees of the *ficus* kind, and passed one mass of trees with bright red foliage.

31 March, Tue. Senafe. A short march. 9 miles. Scenery more like Simla now, but on the top of the pass it is quite different. The reddish stones make it more like central India.

General Stewart has arrived and is now in command at Senafe. He is accompanied by Captain H. Fellowes as Brigade Major. Lieutenant Beck* is Deputy Assistant Quarter Master General. Major Thacker* is Deputy Assistant Com. General. The Head Quarters and three companies of the 21st. Punjab Native Infantry [are] commanded by Major Thelwall C. B.* Four companies of the 10th Bombay Native Infantry, one company of the 21st Bombay Native Infantry, No. 1 Company Bombay Native Artillery, and one troop of the 10th and 12th Bombay Cavalry, are quartered at Senafe.

The 10th and 12th Bengal Cavalry are men from the Punjaub, Sikhs and Patáns, and are two very fine regiments. Their equipment and appearance is very complete. The Bengal Brigade, from more experience in war, have made their appearance in this country in a much more efficient state than the others. When they arrived at Annesley Bay they were ready to land with their commissariat, transport, and every department complete. They were ready on reaching the land to march to the front, and could have faced the enemy at once. This is a state of organization which only time and experience can produce, particularly with Indian troops where so many accessories are necessary.

Many of the Regiments when they landed wanted for almost everything till they were supplied at Zoulla. The great difficulty of war is not the fighting, all men are brave, it is the organisation of the Army, and particularly the keeping up of the supplies. This has been particularly the case in the Abyssinian war, as yet no enemy has been seen. Hunger has been the only adversary that has been in the field, and the only fight has been to face that restless and insatiable foe. The commissariat is the great backbone of an army, and if it and all its allied departments are in good working order, the fighting may be called the holiday of the Army. This, although perhaps not the usual idea of war, is what all true soldiers of experience would admit to be a not unfair statement of the case.

On arriving at Senafe the Expedition was said to have reached "the tableland" of Abyssinia, and this tableland was much talked about at the time. The words suggested a flat country, like the top of a table, to those who were not familiar with the meaning of the geographical phrase. As the Expedition advanced, mountains were found standing upon this tableland, many of them high, peaked, and fantastic in their shapes. Two of the Naval Brigade were heard discussing this subject. One was heard to say: "I believe, Bill, they call this the tableland of Abyssinia." Then, pointing to some high peaks, he added: "Blowed, but they must have turned the table upside down, and them's the legs!" (*Autobiography*, 190)

According to accounts from the front, the Headquarters and advanced troops are without tents and no baggage, pushing on to finish the business. If Theodore made any stand it was expected that it would be at the river Bashilo which is the last to cross before Magdala. As yet there is no news of any opposition by Theodore.

A later story has come in, that Theodore has taken the irons off Rassam, and sent him a friendly letter with a large amount of dollars and fifty cows.[2-12] This last report is from a more reliable authority than the others, and from the channel it comes through it is receiving credit at Senafe.

1 April, Wed. Goun-Gouna. Sent off 6 sketches to-day. At Goun-Gouna saw a church in a cleft of the rock very high up. Mr. Goode* [is] C.O. Goun-Gouna.[2-13]

The way leads from Senafe past the end of the strange-looking rocks which stand up in bare masses with scarce a blade of verdure on them. There are caves and hollows all about them, which would exactly suit the ideas of the monks of the first centuries. I know nothing of the history of Senafe, but if the monkish system of Egypt extended as far south as Abyssinia, these bare rocks must have had tenants in their caves. There is on the top of the highest rock still a church, which would help to confirm this notion. At present the principal occupiers of these rocks are the "dog faced" baboons. This baboon is a very large brute with a mane of splendid hair like a lion. Being now on the plateau, there are [sic] lots of flat land. One a few miles from Senafe is called "Goose plain," another locality in the pass below is known by the name "Guinea fowl vale." I need not explain that these are among the latest importations to the mixed language of Habesh, which is the name by which the country is known and is said to signify a mixture, from the variety of races here.[2-14]

There is now on this high land something like fields and a cultivation going on; droves of cattle, with goats and sheep, and almost always a few donkeys in the flocks, may be seen all over the plain; but at this season from the want of rain every thing is dry and burnt up. In some cases the fields seem prepared for seed. Here and there also a plough may be seen at work, but often one sees a number of natives with a stick digging up a small kind of tuber which produces a grass that is peculiar to this part of the world. These tubers are about the size of peas and very pleasant to eat. They are in great quantities and are eagerly sought for by the poor who seem as if they could easily at any time get a dinner by becoming something like hogs, which a group of them thus engaged very much resembles. It indicates a great deal of poverty which it is difficult to account for in a country with so much land which seems to be in cultivation. There had been a famine for two years owing to bad crops.[2-15]

Goun-Goona is a lovely little valley with green fields and a waterfall at the head of it. There are channels of irrigation here along the fields.[2-16] There is a village here and in a cleft in the rock above the village there is a small church. The face of the rock is quite perpendicular and it must be difficult of access.[2-17]

1 April, Wed. The post leaves this [place] to-day. There was a "Shame" [rumour] from the front last night but it is so doubtful it is scarce worth relating, but as it is the only news, I had better give it.—According to this story Sir Robert Napier was in Magdala, and had got the prisoners and some wives of Theodore, who had fled, direction not given. The story is not quite impossible, for Theodore is so put to straits that it is difficult to see what else he can do.

2 April, Thur. Focada. This is a long march [to Focada], said to be about 18 or 19 miles. On leaving the valley at Goun-Gouna you rise to the top of a long plain with a fine view of the Adowa peaks to the south west. They are a little fantastic. From a valley on the right a few miles from Focada there is a very grand view of these peaks. At Focada there is a village and a church dedicated to Miriam (the Virgin). Behind the village is a high hill formed of basaltic, columnar rocks. There is but a small station at this place, under the command of Captain Beaumont.* There is an hospital for sick mules, under the charge of Veterinary Surgeon Wilson.

3 April, Friday. Adigerat. A beautiful march to-day. Saw mistletoe on the trees. Colonel Little,* Commanding Officer, Adigerat.[2-18]

The march here is about 11 or 12 miles, with a difficult Ghat [pass, defile] to come down about half way. From this Ghat the road passes over a large plain about four miles long, which seems well cultivated, and the young green crops are in some instances several inches above the ground.[2-19]

> This place..is about forty miles from Senafe. It is on an eminence in a plain, surrounded on all sides by high hills, those on the south and west being very lofty. None of them are near enough to command the position, which was fortified on account of its nearness to Adowa, the capital of Tegray, whose Prince, although friendly, might change his polity towards us if any misfortune should chance to occur.

> This is an important point on the line of march, which must be held secure in order to keep up the perpetual current of supplies to the front. The southern and western side of the position is naturally protected by rocks, so that it only required an embankment of earth on the eastern slope and at the northern end. Two Armstrong guns[2-20] are in the camp, and a company of artillery; the 25th Bombay Native Light Infantry form the garrison, under Lieutenant-Colonel Little, who is the commanding officer of the station. Lieutenant Poole is staff officer, Captain Newport has charge of the commissariat, and Captain Christie is the engineer officer. General Malcolm, C.B.,* who commands the second division, was in command here himself until the end of March, when he advanced forward to Antalo to which station his command extends....Adigerat seems a very healthy station, and a plentiful supply of water flows past the northern end of the intrenchment.

Three sutlers' shops [small vendors] have managed to advance thus far into the country, and this advance is accompanied by a wonderful advance in prices. Brandy is quoted at 16s. a bottle; lucifer matches, 1s. a box, the same as sold in the streets of London a a halfpenny. Red herrings may be had at 1s. a piece. These quotations will give an idea of what things cost at Adigerat. One of the sutlers is a Bombay parsee [Zoroastrian]; another shop is kept by two Germans from Cracow. (*ILN*, published 9 May 1868)

At Adigerat there is a village with a church on a rock in the centre of it.[2-21]

A large house stands on the plain, the largest building I have yet seen in the country. It is surrounded by a long wall and contains a number of small houses within. It is said to be the residence of a Princess whose husband is a prisoner in the hands of Kasa, the Tegray Prince.[2-22] I met some of her sons at the church on Palm Sunday. One of them was a very nice young boy, but I think he was a son by another wife, such things seemingly being one of the customs of the country, for this chief had according to report three or four wives.

There are beautiful groves of trees here and there in this part of the country and in most of them there is a church, and these churches have no wall round them like those in the villages. It was owing to this unprotected state that I managed with some others who were with me to enter and inspect the whole of the inside of the Holy of Holies. There is another grove to the west of this with a church dedicated to St John, or as they call him here, [Qeddus] Iannus [Yohannes].

There is a monastery not far from this with a few monks in it. The population of this locality seems to be large. From the top of the camp here we can see numerous villages and churches in every direction, and there is a weekly market at Adigerat where they come in to dispose of their produce. They bring in grass to the [British] commissariat, and a little grain and barley, a few sheep may be had, all the beef of the commissariat is got here, for cattle are plentiful, and although small, they are very good. A great deal of the transport is done by the natives, men and more particularly women carry bags along the road, and native oxen are used as well as mules, so that the Transport corps are not required to be so large here as they otherwise would be.

Recalling the Expedition's transport problems, and the important contribution made by mules, virtually all of which were imported from abroad, Simpson later observed:

The movement towards the interior had begun as early as January, but it was found difficult to march troops through a country that could provide no supplies, or, at any rate, very few. The sending of everything from the Red Sea became a hard task. The farther the troops went the [more the] difficulties increased.

Mules had to be brought from all parts—India, Egypt, Syria, Spain, or wherever they could be found. The mule, with its pack-saddle, became an all-important subject of reports, opinions, and speculations. In fact, it became a sort of sacred animal. Had the Abyssinian Expedition occurred two or three thousand years earlier I believe the mule would have been worshipped, and myths would have arisen as to how it fed a whole army of soldiers, like the wondrous cow in Brahminic mythology.[2-23] (*Autobiography,* 189)

4 April, Sat. Adigerat. Made a halt to-day. The doctor of the 25th B.L.I. [Bombay Native Light Infantry] gave a chief here a bit of ointment for a sore leg, but he put it on his head.

5 April, Sun. Adigerat. Being Palm Sunday, I made another day's halt to see the ceremony in the church.

Simpson "waited a day to see the ceremonies of Palm Sunday. Figure subjects were wanted, and this gave me good material, for I was sending home sketches of what I came upon on the way to the front." *He later describes his experiences:*

On Palm Sunday I went to the church of Adigerat, and was fortunate enough to get the interpreter of the camp with me, who was an Abyssinian; and although speaking English, and in European costume, still professed his adherence to the religion of his own country. He seemed well acquainted with everything relating to the forms of the service, and I am indebted to him for the most of the details here given.

THE ABYSSINIAN CHURCH FESTIVAL OF PALM SUNDAY

59

Palm Sunday is of course one of their great days; the service had begun before day-break (at least the psalm-singing had), and it was not finished when I left between eight and nine o'clock.

Palms were distributed by the priests, and they made no exception with me. After the palms were distributed the priests came out at the front door; a large book was borne by two deacons, a large cross carried, incense and a hand-bell were used, and each had his palm branch. A portion of the book was read—I think the Gospels a psalm sung, and then the procession moved around to the women's door, going through the same ceremony, to the built-up door on the east, and finished at the Beatalehem on the north.[2-24] I could notice no difference in the service at each of these four doors.

The reader, who held a small cross up between him and the book as he read, often came to a pause, and could not go on till he was prompted by those around. At times they stopped him to correct a word, and I noticed that the correction was always adopted. Whether he was an average or exceptional specimen of the priesthood I could not tell, but the incident does not say much for their scholarship.

Of the character of the priesthood my experience is small. A late Abuna [2-25] is reported to have kept up a thriving business in slaves, and although bound to celibacy, he is credited with having had a well-filled harem, some of its inmates being nuns. ("Jottings," 610)

[See also Appendix B for a longer description]

PART III: ADIGERAT TO ANTALO
6 April to 10 April

6 April. Mon. Mai Wahiz [River Wahiz]. Came on here today and dined with the officers of the 45th and Captain Kodolitsch[3-1] of the Austrian Army. Thunder and clouds on the summit of Mount Alika. Rock-cut caves on the way.

There is no news from the front. Everyone is anxious to know the result, as the Advance must be now in close proximity to Magdala. There are occasional showers of rain, at times heavy falls with thunder. One letter from the front reports that it is so cold there, that the Thermometer fell as low as 19°. This must be very trying to them with the light kit [personal effects] they are known to have in the extreme front.

This march is said to be 15 miles to the south of Adigerat in a range of very high mountains, and the route goes round their eastern flank. It is generally very clear in the morning but about midday the clouds gather and rain has been the result. As we passed the end of this higher mass of mountains the clouds had gathered round their tops and came down their sides while a continued growl was going on above. In England we have the peals of thunder, but in the East it is one continued rumble of noise, bursting out louder as it rolls near to you. It was evident that the rain was falling, but it kept clear of our party. When I got round the corner of the spur a long vista of distance opened and I sat down to shelter, but large drops soon began to fall and a recourse to water proof covering became necessary.

As the rain cleared off I found some caves on my left hand, which indicated the labour of human hands. These seemed to confirm the idea that the old monkish system of the Thebiad had extended as far as Abyssinia.[3-2] As I neared the Station water appeared, although small in quantity, yet it was a running stream, and green fields was the result.

There was no town visible at Mai Wahiz, only a few tents under the charge of a Duffadar [non-commissioned officer, Indian army] of the 12th Bengal Cavalry and a few of the men of that regiment. Two Companies of the 45th

Regiment under the command of Major Griffiths* had just arrived, en route for the front. The day before, Captain Kodolitsch of the Austrian Army and the Count Kielmansegge[3-3] of the Austrian Navy arrived at Adigerat, being sent out by the War department of the Austrian Government to report upon the war operations in Abyssinia. Unfortunately Count Kielmansegge was unable to go on, a slight illness made a rest at Adigerat necessary and from the kindness I received there I know he is in good hands. Captain Kodolitsch and I arranged to proceed to the front together, and as he started before me, I found him at Mai Wahiz on my arrival. (Captain Kodolitsch was A.D.C. to Emperor Maximilian, and went through all the events and misfortunes of the empire in Mexico.[3-4]) We dined with the officers of the 45th

> Kodolitsch....had a servant, a quaint fellow named "Joseph" who spoke nothing but German. Kodolitsch himself spoke good English. We got on very well all through the journey, and were of use to each other, because at some of the stations there were no European officers, only a native duffadar, with a few sowars [Privates, Indian army], generally from one of the Sikh irregular corps. As Hindostani only was spoken in such cases, I had to become interpreter. On the other hand, with my two wretched Hindostani servants "Joseph" became a useful addition; he could cook and do everything. (*Autobiography*, 189)

7 April, Tues. Ad Abaga. This is a long march about 16 to 17 miles. We descended a Ghaut and came upon a long plain. In the rocks on the eastern margin we found a good many villages with trees and green fields about them. And it was here that we visited the House of Refuge of which I send a sketch and description.

As we passed along the plain the sun was right over head, but as the clouds began to gather we got a little shade. We passed some large villages, and villages in ruins. The ruins and walls with loop holes round that we passed were very clear indications of the accidents to which property is liable in this part of the world. In addition to a rebellious chief here at times, and the necessary war to bring him to subjection, there are the Gallas, a large tribe on the East and South whose custom it is to make raids on this part of

Abyssinia.**3-5** These are the causes for the peculiar village architecture which is visible in this part of the country.

By a smart ride we got into Ad Abaga in time to save the storm which we saw brewing. The thunder performed its continuous tune, while rain came down in a heavy shower of large drops with hailstones. The 45th were caught in it and came in wet to the skin. The rain put out all the fires in the camp so that a cup of tea which was preparing became an impossibility.

HOUSE OF REFUGE AND DEFENCE AND DWELLING HOUSE IN THE PROVINCE OF TEGRAY

The House of Refuge is built upon a rock that is detached, but resting on the mass to which it originally belonged. The door is about five feet above the rock, and there is a descent of about the same number of feet from the level of the top. The face of the house is full of holes for firing musquets through, so that any one attacking the place, could only get at it from the level ground on the top which would be swept by the fire from these loopholes.

From the plan of the place it will be seen that the dwelling house and the still larger house for the beasts of the field have both their doors in such a position that they are commanded by the fire from the House of Refuge.

The conclusion I came to was that if attacked they would put all the cattle and other animals into the house on the left, perhaps a few into the enclosure, if the house would not hold them all, and that all the family would take shelter in the fortified building, leaving their household utensils in the dwelling. If this were done all their worldly goods and themselves would thus be in a state of almost perfect safety. If the enemy were to try to enter any of the houses to carry off the cattle or property they would have to run the gauntlet of a musquetry fire both entering and leaving.

They showed us two guns in the place of refuge. One was a tolerably good article but the other was fired by a match.**3-6** Still they would be sufficient to resist any attack, and the whole arrangement would indicate a liability to marauding invaders, which would be only of short duration. If this is the correct conclusion it indicates a state bordering close upon absolute anarchy, and this is confirmed from the fact that the Tegray Prince [Dajazmach Kasa] is at present out in a large camp to coerce one of his subject chiefs into obedience. While such a petty civil war is going on the commissariat arrangements of the contending forces may be very easily guessed at by the plan of this place of refuge and defence: It indicates that

> He will take who has the power,
> And he will keep who can.

They evidently have no fear of those belonging to the present invasion of Abyssinia [the British], for upon reaching the place they came forward and received us with a "Salaam" and the most perfect confidence, and allowed us to enter and inspect the whole of the place.

I send you a small plan of what seemed the dwelling house, or rather it might be their kitchen for the sleeping space did not seem large enough for the inmates, so I am inclined to think, that the place of refugee would be the general night quarters.

When we entered the dwelling the principal woman of the party was asleep upon the place which [I] have named the bed in the plan. Her pillow [traditional headrest] reminded me of those used by the ancient Egyptians.

The house was round, and about 15 feet in diameter with a conical thatched roof—which is seen, as well as the roof of the house for cattle, in the view—supported by a central pole. On the left in entering was the place where the woman was resting. On the right were two fire places with round pans of iron, slightly hollowed with iron covers to them. These were for baking their bread and cooking. Behind these was a place for grinding grain; there was another place for the same purpose, and each of these places had two stones, so that four grinders could be at work at one time. The whole place was full of jars of all sizes, some of them being very large, and wooden platters and baskets of various shapes made of straw. Some of these baskets are really beautifully made and are the only specimens of workmanship of any value that I have yet seen in this country.

The woman who appeared to be the mistress of the house rose on our entrance, and after a few minutes we heard the word *lokomo,* which means something to eat, and is one of the words in common use between us and the natives.[3-7] On looking round the woman had a wooden platter with small lumps of dough and ghee, for they have no butter here. She inserted a small bit of wood into one of the lumps and dipping it into some red pepper, presented it to us eat. It tasted cold and very insipid. I ate a couple of them and we declared them to be *malkám,* the word used here for good.

By this time the place had got full of children and all the household. The little ones stood on platters and bowls to see me sketching, and an addition of fuel to the fires so filled the house with smoke, the chimney being the holes in the thatch, [that] I was obliged to retreat before I could get all done that I wanted.

The family relationship in this household I could not make out, the want of the language preventing all explanation, and even much of what I here state is given as only my own conclusion formed from what I saw on the spot. There were a great number of children of all ages, and besides the woman who seemed the mistress there were two women who had babies.

We only saw one man and a grown-up boy, and the man did not seem to be old enough to be the husband of the principal woman.

The man and the boy were engaged [in] reading on the top of the rocks. The books were in manuscript and bound, with leather cases to preserve them. The cultivation of literature seemed at strange variance with the rude state of existence indicated by all the circumstances of the place.

WOMAN GRINDING GRAIN—PROVINCE OF TEGRAY

This sketch [page 67] will shew the mode of grinding grain as it was done in the houses just described. The process was performed by rubbing the grain between two stones, somewhat similar to the way on which colours are ground with a slab and muller. The lower stone seemed worn into a curve by long grinding. The place in which the stone stood was formed of a mass of mud with a ledge all round, and a hole at the end of the stone for receiving the flour when it is ground.

The seeds the woman was grinding were very small and they were first toasted on the pan. The woman had a cotton petticoat and a leather upper garment decorated with two or three rows of cowries.[3-8] In this leather dress she carried the baby on her back. In this part [of the country] the women plait their hair in rows in various ways over the head.

There was one girl employed in grinding who was blind. She stopped her work and stood listening, with the most earnest attention, using those senses which she had left, and which are said to be more sensitive from the absence of any of the other faculties. She looked to our eyes to be about fifteen or sixteen years of age, and although she saw nothing, yet our visit seemed a bit of light in her dark monotonous life.

I wished to have given more of this household, but was unable to do so. So I must illustrate the domestic life of the people from other localities which I may visit, and this may give me varieties of their life, so that if one has made mistakes in this one case they may be corrected by others.

8 April, Wed. Dongolo. As this was a short march and the next one was also short, we made it a double march.

8 April. Agoola. The whole character of the country has again changed. Instead of the high table topped rocks about Adigerat and Mai Wahiz, we have now low uninteresting hills with plains between, covered with stones and small trees or brush, with here and there a village and a plough at work.[3-9] Occasionally there is a running stream, but it is a very feeble effort in that sort of thing.

Water does not remain in this part of the world, it is either carried off by the rapid slopes of the mountains, or absorbed by the ground in the dry air. The scarcity of water as an irrigator seems to have something to do with the passivity and poverty of the country. Water is a great civiliser. England does not want for moisture and she is not among the least of the nations. It was

67

irrigation that made Babylon and Nineveh great. Now that part of the world is a desert. The canals are mounds of earth, and the population are little better than robbers. It was the water of the Nile that built the pyramids of Egypt, and Egypt has always been great in proportion to the canals which utilize the waters of the Nile.

It was the want of water [which] caused the late famine in Orrissa,[3-10] and a liability to such famines must end in the destruction of all government and lead to chaos. According to Scripture, and all the mythologies of the ancients repeat the same idea, it was out of water that Creation or Cosmos came in, and it is not only a physical but at the same time a moral and political truth that Cosmos or order requires a due allowance of water or humidity for its realization. Irrigation is one of the wants of the country and works of that kind would be the real antidotes to such absolutism as that of Teodorus, or the anarchy and burglar-like invasions of such tribes as the Gallas.

There is the remains of an old church at Agoola, and from its plan I conclude that it belonged to the Abyssinian church.[3-11] It has been a well built edifice, with stone pillars, and a few small fragments of ornament remain.

Clouds and thunder in the afternoon, but we were lucky in escaping the rain. There was a bright lunar rainbow to-night when the moon rose. The lightning later struck the telegraph wire and melted it, causing a stoppage in the messages.

9 April, Thursday. Dolo. This is a very long and heavy march, up and down hills with very many stones on the way. It was impossible to clear off all the stones for such a distance as this road extends, but wherever there was a rock in the road it has been cleared out of the way, and in some cases heights have been scaled by a good new zig-zag. The sides of hills have been leveled and on the whole a fair road is visible as far as I have yet gone, which contrasts in a very palpable manner with the mountainous paths of the country. War is not supposed to be a civiliser, but in this case the making of this road will certainly convert the present war [i.e. that of the British Expedition] from its usual results into an agent of progress and a great benefit to the inhabitants of the country.

When the Queen of Sheba came to Jerusalem to try Solomon with hard questions, this must have been her route, and she must have had a good deal of hard jolting on the way with her "Great Train" as she crossed these rough stony passes. Had she come along the road at the present moment she might have found a few more hard questions with which to puzzle that wisdom whose fame had extended all over the east. That slender issue that extends from port to port along the line of route might be mentioned as one of those hard questions, of which many more might be found in the present expedition.

That peculiar manifestation of female virtue which gave birth to the Abyssinian race has not yet left the dark daughters of the race of Sheba's Queen, but that curiosity which took her [on] such a far journey as Jerusalem has entirely disappeared, for with the exception of a great desire to know if you are a Christian they seem perfectly indifferent to everything that goes on. At every station there is a large colony of them living on the borders of the camp in rude huts, and they prowl about gathering up all the refuse so as to get the few bits of grain that fall from the horses' food, that with any other scraps they can pick up in their *lokomo* which may be truly called Grub. This with their digging in herds into the ground for roots makes them rank about as low as the scavenger dogs of Constantinople or the Pariah pigs of an Indian village.

Our route is yet on the high ground forming the watershed between the Red Sea and the Nile. We have passed places where there was only a narrow ridge where two drops of water might be seen departing: one for the Atlantic and the other for the Indian Ocean, with no chance of ever meeting except at the Cape of Good Hope or Cape Horn.

10 April, Friday. Eikhullet, 9 miles; as this was a short march we determined to go on the next to Antalo.

10 April. Antalo.[3-12] All the stations from Adigerat are small places, with no commissariat except grain and grass for horses. They are all in charge of Duffadars of the 12th Bengal Cavalry, who are Punjaubees, and they have been the most obliging and attentive to us while passing along.

Antalo is a large Station with a Divisional General and a Brigadier General in command, and a good force of troops. Those we have at present: four Companies of the 45th Regiment, one troop 10th Bengal Cavalry, 50 sabres of the 12th Bengal Cavalry, 2 companies 25th Native Infantry, 3 companies of 3rd Native Infantry, one company of Sappers and Miners, and there is en route 5/25 Battery Royal Artillery, [and] one troop of 10th Bengal Cavalry. General Malcolm C.B. arrived two days ago. The Brigade command is under General Collings.* Major Quin* is Brigadier Major. Lieutenant de Thoren* is Assistant Quarter Master General, and Captain Bally* is A.D.C.

We find here alarms of all sorts from attacks by the natives. They attacked a medical officer marching alone to his station, a sapper has also been severely wounded by them, and they attacked and wounded two men of the 3rd Bombay Cavalry, carrying off their horses and arms. From this no one is allowed to go above half a mile from the camp, and we will not be able to proceed without an escort, but luckily there is a quantity of treasure going up to the front with a strong escort, and we go with it in all likelihood tomorrow the 11th.

This being Good Friday I was very anxious to [see] the ceremonies of the Abyssinian Church if I could have found one, but no one was near, and the double march made it impossible for me to go on the hunt for such a place, and from the temper manifested by the natives here it is perhaps as well that I did not wander from the line of route. I met one young fellow who took a piece of bread out of his dress and pointing to it said it was "Christian" and offered it to me to eat. From what he said I came to the conclusion that he had got it in church and that it was the Abyssinian Hot Cross Bun. There were marks on it which may have been that of a Cross, but the fragment was too small to speak of it with certainty. I broke a piece off and ate it. It was grey in colour and it tasted as if it were composed of more than one kind of flour, of which one I thought to be made from peas.

An officer here has just told me what he saw at the church in the village here, but it is about the same as the ceremony of reading the Bible at Adigerat only that they did not read at the four sides of the church, and they rung a bell going four times round the building while doing so. They are in the custom here also of putting up a rude figure or doll to represent the Crucifixion.

Still no news of the end of the Expedition. There are very great difficulties in the way. It took one day to advance five miles. The whole army was employed in forming a road.

PART IV: **ANTALO TO LAT**
                     11–15 APRIL

11 April, Sat. Antalo. A letter from the front this morning reporting that Theodore had visited Prideaux* and another of the prisoners, and that [he] had been very courteous and civil to them. The conclusion come to here is that he is anxious [to] make things smooth.

11 April. Mashik. This [is] a double march of about 17 miles, Masgeh [Masgee] being the station half way. The camp at Antalo stands in the middle of an undulating plain with high hills on the West and the South. There is a large village at Antalo with a weekly fair or market. From the uncertain state of the roads the authorities at Antalo thought it as well that we should proceed along with some treasure, doing so with a strong escort [composed] of the 12th Bombay Cavalry and the 3rd Bombay Cavalry.

On our way we passed many ruined villages telling the usual story of raid and rapine. These roofless walls in this part are said to be some of Theodore's work. At Masgeh there is a running stream with a spring of fine clear cold water, the finest water I have drunk since I came to this country and it is in the most plentiful supply.

From Masgeh our route led up a valley among the hills, which were very fine in their outline and in some places grand from the great masses of perpendicular rock. The narrow irregular strips at the bottom of the valley or ravine, for it was little else, the crops [were] cultivated with small fields irrigated by channels. Some of the crops were green, some yellow and at one place the crop was cut, and they were threshing out the grain with sticks. At last the path reached the level of the stream, and led through small grass meadows over which the road went repeatedly crossing the running water, and passing under masses of foliage, with flowering trees and plants.[4-1] One of the common flowers is a sort of white wild rose which was in great quantities in this glen. The water is fringed by long stalks of mint in flower which with other plants scented the air.

This has certainly been the most pleasant spot we have yet passed in Abyssinia. The small Station, of one bell tent, was at the head of this sylvan brook, under a group of what looked like willow trees, at whose roots the water flowed out. We ate our dinner stretched out on the grass round the light of the fire which had cooked it, and then to bed with a tree for our tent, over which by and by the moon passed, and with the greater light of the morning we were up and on our way.

From Antalo we had to take 15 days provisions with us—no tea or sugar being now allowed. From Adigerat the most of the transport is done by the natives and from Antalo it is almost wholly so. The Easter ceremonies have rather interfered with this work and with that of bringing in grain and grass to the different stations.

12 April, Easter Sunday. Attala. I tried to learn about the ceremonies of the Abyssinian Church on this day and was told by the interpreter of Antalo that they would be all over by four o'clock in the morning and that the rest of the day would be spent in feasting in their houses. By four o'clock the sacrament would be celebrated. So I gave up all idea of seeing anything of it.

The route led up the same ravine of yesterday, and at last we had to climb up the side of the hill to get over a pass, which is on the eastern flank of a very remarkable peak called "Amba Alaje," or Mount Alajé. It was a very steep ascent, and the descent was equally so on the southern side. It was in the descent and while resting I made friends with the natives who were robbed and beaten, and with the two Sikh Sowars who made the capture. We found the camp in the middle of the plain below. This plain had evidently at some early period been a lake. There was a good stream and some bright green fields. While having a bath I found water cresses in the running water. There were many flowers along the bank, mint in great quantities, and another flower, common in such places at home, was the *Veronica Beccabunga*. Every march now brings us among more flowers. In the pass we came over there was a gigantic thistle which grew in some cases as high as 12 or 13 feet, one would have dined two or three donkeys.[4-2]

13 April, Mon. Bulago. This march has been very variously estimated from 7 to 10 miles, but as it contains two ascents and descents over two passes the length is scarcely a fair way of forming an idea of the labour to be gone through in the march. High above us on the second pass was a very high mountain, which from the map I should take to be Debra Mousa. On one of its lower ridges of rock we saw a few houses which seemed perfectly inaccessible, fit only for birds and monkeys. Some of them seemed hollow ridges in the rocks. We heard voices still higher up but could see no one. We were told that this was the place where the two men of the 3rd Bombay Cavalry were attacked and their horses and arms carried off. From what the Sowars said who were with us, these people were nothing less than "Loose-wallahs" or robbers, and if their plans are to pounce down upon travellers and either rob or levy blackmail, no locality could be better arranged for their purpose.

13 April. Makan. As this was only about 6 miles farther we went on the same day. We descended still farther into a fine large vale or rather a plain of some four or five miles extent in any direction surrounded by hills. On our right at Bulago, we passed a ruined village; and as we came down on the plain I found a large village on my left on the top of a small eminence. I looked with my glass but could see no one in the village. I passed close enough to see the pieces of wood of which the houses were formed, but although I used my glass repeatedly I could see nothing of life in it, and no one was to be seen in the fields neither men cultivating nor herds of cattle. There were fields on terraces everywhere [but] a perfect stillness reigned.

I happened to ride on in advance and the path was very beautiful, wandering among trees and flowers. Birds of all kinds were singing and flying about. As I got further into the plain I saw more villages on the crests of hills but they were too far away to tell whether they were inhabited or not. The total absence of all appearance of cultivation in the fields of this beautiful plain belied the existence of any population. The only conclusion was that it illustrated the line:

> Man makes a desert and calls it peace.[4-3]

But a change soon came over the scene. Captain Kodolitsch had just made up to me as I was leaving the plain by the pass at its southern extremity, and if Roderick Dhu had given the signal the transformation could not have been more complete.[4-4] We heard a loud noise and then the points of spears appeared among the bushes. Soon the dark heads of men burst out in a noisy crowd, and came rushing forward seemingly in a countless multitude.

We had come on in advance from the last Station with our baggage and an escort of only three Sowars of the 3rd Bombay Cavalry. So we knew we were helpless in such a case if attack were intended, but we instinctively felt that a shew of confidence was the only tactic.

We had just expressed this plan of action when they were upon us, and all further consideration became unnecessary, for it was evident they were friends. They called out "Sultan" to us which is a title of respect they use to Europeans similar to the Hindustani "sahib."[4-5] Then "Christian," and "tayib," the word for good. They were all armed with spears and swords. Many had shields and a few had musquets, or rather what was intended for such, for many of them reminded one of their youthful attempts with an old key tied to a stick by which most boys have at one time or another endeavoured to produce something like fire arms. On they came, mass after mass of them, with noise and shouting, chiefs with their long shawl and its broad red stripe, the great mark of rank in this country. All as they passed called out the three words "Sultan," "Christian," "tayib," to us and went on into the valley we had just left. Their purpose or place of march we could not make out.

At last in the midst of a greater crowd than usual we saw the chief of the whole coming forward. He did not seem much different from the rest except that he rode and had some red silk in his costume. The plaited hair of [his] head and the dark colour of his face was the same as his followers. He smiled, and Captain Kodolitsch pressed into the crowd with his horse and shook hands. When they had all passed we tried to estimate the number that had passed us and we agreed that it could not have been much less than one thousand men. What was their object of their expedition we could not make out. Was it peace or war? Was that mass of people only the guard of the chief we saw, on some peaceful visit? To the country through which they passed it would make little difference whether they were friends or foes. We saw no baggage. The civil and military costume of each man was on his back, and the commissariat would be found wherever they went. Dugald Dulgetty's plan of quartering upon the enemy was evidently their system,[4-6] and its results might be seen in the desolate country we had passed through.

The Inspector in charge of the treasure, when he met them after passing us, thought he was about to be looted when he saw the mass of men coming towards him, and he formed up his escort in line of battle, but they passed on calling out the same words which they did with us. Who they were we have as yet been unable to find out.

14 April, Tues. Ashangi. The march is said to be 13 miles, but it seemed to us a little longer. It has been the finest march we have had, or rather it is the finest piece of country we have passed through. Fields, hills and mountains, and all beautifully wooded, but the fields were green only with grass, no cultivation, and no people. I believe that this is the border land close to the country of the Gallas and that is the reason of the desolation so evident all round. About the middle of the march we had to go over a pass, and when we reached the top of it we looked down on the lake, which was one of the most pleasant sights I have seen on the way. The word *Talaad*, Hindustanee, means a tank or a lake.[4-7] If it has any connection with the Greek "talazza" is more than I know, but it was very striking to hear every Hindoo as he reached the top of the pass exclaim "*Talaad! Talaad!*"

Water to all Easterns is of great value, and to the Hindoo it is of the very highest importance. I heard them all talk of having a bath, but the camp, when we reached it, was a long way from the water, and I fear few of them managed to get a wash. There is a good deal of flat land which evidently has been at one time [a] lake, and on this, close to the foot of the mountain, the camp of Ashangi is pitched.

On coming over the pass before mentioned, a very palpable change was evident. On a hill underneath was a village and we could hear the sounds of life—upon another hill there was a village and there also we could see and hear that it was inhabited—and when we reached the plain which the waters of Lake Ashangi had left we found it alive with ploughs, and the population seemed to be large. There were crops in all stages. Some where the plough was passing over the soil, some where the young leaf only was visible, and in others the grain was formed, and I saw what seemed barley quite ripe, ready for taking in, and as I neared the camp I saw a number of natives hard at work threshing out the grain. This was the same as I had seen on the march from Mashik to Attala only on a much larger scale. The lower parts of the hills are covered with villages, and the outskirts of the camp is busy with natives, all so different from the country we have just passed through.

Lake Ashangi is said to be 7500 feet above the sea, and about four miles by three in extent. That is a large sheet of water to be so high above the ocean, but the Choomoreree in Ladok [Ladakh] is 5500 ft. high, which is quite equal to the height of Mount Blanc, and is about twenty miles in length.

The only news to give from this place is what goes by the name of "The Battle of Ashangi." There is a weekly fair held here on every Monday, and on Monday week, a party of people came down to stop the selling of grain to the camp. The poor people are willing to sell their grain, but it was the chiefs who wanted to stop the traffic. Now, it is this bringing in of grain by the natives, which keeps the Station camps in food, and supporting the transport of all things to the front; without this all transport would eat up more than it carries to Head quarters. This attempt to stop the sale of grain caused what is perhaps best expressed by the word "row," and the result was, that one native was killed and five were wounded. This interference all along the line of communication, although manifested in different ways, has a suspicious look about it. It may be an accident, but I give the facts as I have heard them related. The late "row" has had a very beneficial effect, for since it took place large quantities of grain have come in, and the officer commanding has been able to push on supplies to the front.

As this is rather a large camp I had better give the names of the officers. Major Armstrong* of the 10th Bengal Cavalry is in command. Ensign Porteous* of the 3rd Bombay Cavalry is here having been sent for on account of the "row" or "Battle of Asghangi," whichever name you like. Lieutenant Hore* has been for some time in charge of the Commissariat.

From the pass leading over to Ashangi, we could see far to the east a vast plain, a great deal lower down than the level of the lake. In it large forests were visible and beyond all were a range of mountains. This is the country of the Gallas. They are Mahomedans, and the most of the people at Ashangi are followers of the prophet. They do not enquire as to whether we are

Christians. The lake also goes by the Arabic name of *Tzudo Bahri,* or White Sea.

15 April, Wed. Wofela. This is seven miles from Ashangi. The camp is in the middle of a plain of some miles in extent, and is under the charge of a Duffadar. We found here a Sultan or chief of the Gallas who had come in to offer his good will at the price of sixty [Maria Theresa] dollars, a fair example of that *culte de Dollar* which is supposed to belong exclusively to the West. He was to hasten to Ashangi, and no doubt but if he could support his good will by sending a number of his people to carry stores to the front, the authorities may not be averse to the offering required. This man was very large in stature and stout in body, with a strong sensual expression in his face. He had a sword and spear. His dress was the same as his followers, even more dirty; [with] the red stripe which indicates rank. I would ask the author of the "Vestiarum Christianum" to note the above point in vestments. It was much narrower than in the inferior chiefs, being only about 2 inches while the others were about six or seven broad, and it was not all red, part of it was blue.

On his forehead I noticed some dark spots, and was told that it was goats' blood. The meaning of this, for want of an interpreter, I could not make out. The usual custom here is to put a pat of butter upon the head,[4-8] and it is told of a chief who came to one of our army surgeons with a sore leg, and the box of lard that was prescribed, when given this swell, he at once applied it to the thick plaited locks of his head. Such were his ideas of the use of ointment.

15 April. Lat. We only stopped about half an hour at Wofela, and we came on to this camp. The distance is variously estimated at from 7 to 11 miles. I think it is nearer 11 than 7. There is a very steep ascent from which a distant peep of Ashangi may be got and a long range of the Gallas country can be seen in the extreme distance to the east. It is remarkable to see the villages in this border country how they are stuck up on the very tops of inaccessible peaks, still indicating a Rob Roy population.

As we toiled up the pass a dark cloud had gathered over Ashangi and growls of thunder began to reach our ears, a large cumulus cloud was increasing to great dimensions over our heads, and at last a loud roll of sound began, while away south one heard the same tune upon another key. Slowly all the blue above was closed up and a ceaseless sound was kept up and when we reached the top of the pass it seemed like a grand oratorio going on. The deep loud bass was overhead, while the milder parts of the music were to be heard to the right and the left. It was very fine to be in the thick of this continued rolling and bursting of sound for the pass is about 9000 or 10000 feet high, but the rain began, and soon came down in very large drops which at once destroyed the whole grandeur of the music, for it became a rush to get into Lat which was accomplished before one's clothes were quite drenched.

This station is in the charge of Mr. Mullane* who by cultivating the good graces of the natives manages to get all sorts of supplies from them, some of which he has just brought in to show us. One is a large fruit about as large as a man's head,[4-9] and the other a round cake about eighteen inches in diameter and about an inch and a half thick, richly ornamented with what looks like the "String" ornament of the ancient pre-historic Britons.[4-10]

I have just seen what I take to be a reliable letter, and it would seem that the Commander-in-Chief is now before Magdala, and it is said that Theodore is quite ready to receive us, so heavy fighting is expected. A Reconnoitring Party had been within four miles of Magdala and they report its enormous natural strength.[4-11] They saw Theodore's cavalry, and state that it had a fine appearance and seemed very regular. It was picqueted outside Magdala. Ladders and sandbags are getting ready—which looks as if a siege were expected, or at least an assault of the fortress. This all betokens that Theodore intended to hold out.

That is the substance of the letter; no doubt but I will get clearer information soon as I am now close to the scene of operations.

PART V: LAT TO DALANTA PLAIN
16 to 20 April

LATEST INTELLIGENCE:

16 April, Thurs. Lat. Captain Hodges* of the 76th has just come in with dispatches announcing that on Sunday the 12th Theodore had sent in all the prisoners, sixty-one in all, 138 women and children.[5-1]

On Good Friday the 10th Theodore attacked the baggage and he was met by the 4th King's Own, 23rd Pioneers and the Belooches [Baluchis; 27th Bombay Native Infantry] in the centre. They were repulsed and four hundred were left dead on the field, all the wounded got back to Magdala. Their Head man, the Commander of the forces, Gobervee,[5-2] was found dead on the field.

On Monday if Theodore did not come in himself Magdala would be shelled, Sir Robert Napier being determined to get possession of Theodore's person.[5-3] Theodore tried to shoot himself on Sunday. 18,888 [rounds] of the Snider ammunition were used in the fight.[5-4] On our side there were 28 wounded. The only officer wounded is Mr. Roberts* of the 4th, wounded in the arm. The Abyssinians kept up a fire for three hours and the 23rd Sikh and Pioneers had a charge with the bayonet.

Captain Hodges has been riding with his dispatches for three days and three nights on order to catch the mail. He left Magdala on Monday morning at six o'clock, and the rain made the ground very bad.

16 April. Marawar. I had just sealed my packet this morning to leave it at Lat for the post, when I found that an officer had come in from the front, and I was delighted at the good news. I found Captain Hodges at a very frugal breakfast while a horse was being got ready, and during the few minutes thus engaged I scribbled down a very short summary of the news he brought, which I trust you received [in] a mail sooner than the packet was intended for. Having opened and resealed my letter Captain Hodges finally undertook to see that it would be sent with the same mail that carried the dispatches which were in his charge.

Although with only two hours sleep he expected on the same day to reach Antalo where the telegraph ends and by that means to stop the mail so as to send....[illegible lines]

One of the [messages] related that Theodore had almost two hundred prisoners in Magdala and he caused them to be tied and pitched over the steep rocks which form the natural strength of the fortress. Why he did not do the same with the other prisoners is not yet explained. Amongst our people at the front the betting was that we would not get the prisoners alive. Such would have been the general idea.

As tents and such things as delicacies are scarce at the camp it is said that the released prisoners are complaining of the want of comforts. They had asked for cheroots and something to drink, but those are just the articles which are so scarce, rum being a precious article in the front; for some time it has been almost unknown, and the position of the prisoners in Magdala may be guessed from their saying that if Sir Robert Napier had come into that place he would have been treated in a much better style.

This march is about 13 or 14 miles, a great part of it being a long descent. At Lat there is a good deal of cultivation going on, with green crops in the small terraced fields, and a plentiful supply of very clear water running. As the camp seemed an open place with no shelter and no tents, we agreed to go on and camp in some nice place by the way. This we did and got a very good camping ground about six miles on.

17 April, Fri. Dildi. This is a long march, about 20 miles. There is no good ascent or descent, but a continual up and down. The sides of the hills are covered with fields and villages. At Dildi there is a pretty large camp in charge of Lieut. Warburton.*

18 April, Sat. Wandach. Captain Kodolitsch and I determined to leave our servants and try to do the next few marches with what our horses could carry in addition to ourselves, this being little more than a couple of blankets. By this means we hope to see Magdala before the whole of our people retire from it.

Recalling their efforts at this time to hasten to Magdala, before the Expedition withdrew from it, Simpson later wrote:

The nearer the front we came, the more anxious Kodolitsch and I were to accelerate our movements. My time was not lost on the road, for I was doing figure subjects and sending them home by mail, and that was the main thing the editor demanded of me. (*Autobiography*, 190)

The march to Wandach is said to be 9 miles. It is one continued ascent the whole way, over a narrow stone path with deep precipices on each side. It has been about the hardest climb we have yet had. Instead of referring to the barometer to indicate the height, one should in this expedition express the altitude by the number of dead commissariat mules which such difficult places are sure to produce, and which in any case we found plentiful enough, with huge vultures in numerous attendance performing the part of undertakers. Wandach is a small station with a native Duffadar.

18 April. Takazze River. We only halted a few minutes and then went on. So far [as] we have gone, the steepest sides of the passes have been on the north. The south side of this pass slopes down for about 11 miles and we were able to ride nearly the whole way. About half way down we found a part of the 3rd Bombay Native Infantry under Colonel Campbell* encamped, who kindly gave us some breakfast, and the news of the taking of Magdala and the death of Theodore. Letters had been sent in demanding Theodore to deliver himself up as well as the fortress, and it is understood that messages were sent assuring him of honourable treatment,[5-5] but he replied to none, and on Monday after three hours bombardment an Assault was made and the place was taken. Theodore is said to have been killed at the second gate, and a very large number of his soldiers were there found dead. The Snider rifle seems by its rapid and terrible fire to have frightened them very much.

The people of Dildi expressed their feelings in regard to Theodore by saying that if he were handed over to them, they would not kill him at once, but would begin by cutting bits out of him so as to extend his suffering over a number of days. He seems to have done some very cruel things at Dildi, pinning men to the ground like a raw hide to dry was one of his main processes of painful punishment.

There used to be vines at Dildi but Theodore rooted them all out, so that he might have an exclusive property in grapes from some vineyard of his own.

At the Takazze river we had a bath which gave the horses a rest. The river at this season is very small but we found a pool in which a little swimming could be done. The camp is about a mile above the river on the south side.

18 April. Santara. This is another very hard climb, steep the whole way up the south side of the Takazze valley. We had the afternoon sun upon us, and it was very warm for we did a good deal of it on foot to save the horses. Found the usual quantity of dead mules, making the air foul, and giving the indication of the great height with [illegible] as ascent. On the top is the Wadela plain, which is upwards of 10000 feet high, and the change in temperature was most palpable.**5-6** It blew a bitter cold east wind, and in this we had to ride about a mile over the plateau to the camp. Luckily we got a tent here, and under its shelter it felt cold all night.

19 April, Sun. Gahso. We got up and off very early intending to reach this [place] about 10 o'clock. It is said to be a march of 10 miles. The road is over the undulating top of the plateau, and we found many tracks, so much so that we lost ourselves, and got into a complete bewilderment as to where we were. This was principally owing to our complete ignorance of the Amharic language, for we could neither speak nor understand what was said. After a long ride, and going down some breakneck places, we got a man who seemed to comprehend our plight, and he used the word *Suffer,* and pointed to the path. So we understood that word to be the equivalent to "Road."**5-7** From his action, we thought it best to follow and after some miles of up and down we reached the Station, and learned that many had lost their way as well as ourselves.

19 April. Sindi. After a short rest at Gahso we came on here and got in just before dark. The whole way it seemed to be the top of a high land, undulating with the dried up stony beds of streams here and there. The villages since we passed the Takazzee are built of stone with thatched roofs. They are all round in form. Now there is not that appearance of defence about them which was so manifest about the region of Lake Ashangi. Many of the fields were ploughed and in some the green blade was visible. The quantity of stones on this plateau is very great, suggesting that showers of them must have fell [sic], so thick are they that in a ploughed field you can scarcely see the earth for stones. Sindi is 9500 feet high or about a thousand feet below Santara. We did not find it so cold as it was at the latter place.

20 April, Mon. Bethor. We had scarcely left Sindi this morning when we met the disarmed army of Theodorus coming, forming a very strange mixed multitude of men, women and children. I never saw such a swarm. They streamed down upon a plain of yellow grass like a vast flight of locusts, but it recalled many ideas of vast bodies of men. Here was perhaps a most perfect picture of an Eastern army—I mean of an ancient army such as Genghis Khan or men of that time would have—formed of a mixed multitude all moving along carrying their houses—a few rags and a pole for a tent, carrying their household utensils in the shape of bags and pots with their food, wives, children, servants or slaves as the case may be, women riding mules veiled from head to foot, negro women marching, with scarce a bit of cloth to cover them. There were swells with silk coats, and others with leopard skins. Some—we supposed them wounded in the late fighting— were carried upon men's shoulders on extemporised litters. One man we saw had the main portion of a loom on his pack.

This army was more like a people or a nation moving in some grand emigration, perhaps as the Hebrews might have appeared as they streamed across from the Land of Goshen to the Red Sea.[5-8] We learned afterwards that they were being sent to their homes.

> As the Hebrews crossed the desert, old and young, healthy and sick, slave and free, carrying their kneading-troughs and laden with all the articles of domestic life; some with mules and donkeys covered with baggage of all kinds; so were the people forming this vast exodus—men, women, and children, servants, asses, and mules—all laden with their worldly goods. Wounded chiefs were carried upon litters, while behind them might be seen their wives, who were wrapped in ample sheets, riding with their children. Warriors who had the good fortune not to come in contact with the Snider projectiles might have been seen striding along, their only weapon now being a long staff. With the men of this class it is the custom to wear round the neck a skin of either the sheep, the leopard, or

the lion. Their hair is plaited in five thick rows over the head, and generally well buttered. Silks and rich-coloured cloths were common, contrasting with the slight and simple clothing of those whose position was that of slaves or servants.

It was impossible to estimate the numbers forming this mass, but I am informed that there were about 30,000, of whom about 7000 only were fighting men. They were all on their way to their different homes, and already there is news that they have been attacked and robbed on the way. Probably there were grudges against them, as the soldiers of King Theodore, which had to be paid off. (*ILN*, published 13 June 1868)

To make sure that we would not lose ourselves this morning we got an Abyssinian to act as guide, and he was to see us to the camp at Headquarters. This is from Sindi two marches, and this man took us [by] the road that he would have gone himself, which was no doubt a near cut [shortcut], but when we came to the cliff which overhangs the bed of the Jedda river we saw it was quite out of the question to take our horses down to the place the man seemed to think was a correct and proper road. We now saw that we were as far astray as we had been yesterday morning, and it took us a long time to get back upon a path leading to Bethor.

On our way we passed a very large flock of baboons. As they were of all sizes, old, young, and chiefs of the flock with great manes of hair, and our approach made them swarm away, they seemed not unlike the vast human herd we had so lately seen. The one seemed a sort of caricature of the other, and as they were both so strange, but which was really the caricature it might be hard to say. I might suggest that both were caricatures of humanity.

When we got to the small station at Bethor the Parsee in charge of the Commissariat kindly gave us some breakfast and we started for Headquarters.

20 April, Mon. Dalanta Plain. Between Bethor and the Head quarters on Dalanta Plain[5-9] there is the Jedda River whose bed is upwards of 3000 feet below the plains upon each side, and here on the descent we came upon Theodore's military road, evidently made under the direction of some one who thought he understood European road making.**5-10** It is about 15 feet wide and zig-zags along, but its great defect is that it is too steep for any practical purpose, being in the difficult places about 45 Degrees and a perfect desert of stones. The road was for the purpose of moving Theodore's mortars—now celebrated, and his guns, but how this was done I cannot say. It seemed to me an impossibility. It is almost an impossible road for a horse.

We found an old woman lying upon it, I thought at first dead. Flies were going into her mouth and out again. She seemed perfectly done up. As she lay in the middle of the road there was a way on each side for the Pharisees to pass by, but my friend Capt Kodolitsch performed the part of the good Samaritan by producing his flask and giving the poor creature a drop of rum, and doing all we could to revive her, but I fear it was useless. We had a wash in the Jedda and then the climb up the other side to the Dalanta Plain and arrived at the Headquarters about 5 o'clock. **5-11**

Simpson described his arrival at Napier's headquarters near Magdala and his first sight of the released prisoners:

When we reached the Headquarters it had left Magdala and crossed the Bashilo. From the side of the deep valley of that river the hill fortress was visible, and I made sketches of it. We remained two days before the return march began. The second division marched the morning before we did, and the released prisoners were sent on with it. I saw them start. They were a motley group, to a certain extent a miniature of the released soldiers we had seen a few days before. This was owing to the number of natives attached to them. Some had native wives; there were children and servants of all kinds, male and female. Some carried baskets, pots, pans, and luggage of every description, such as we had seen with Theodore's soldiers. They turned out to be an unruly lot, grumbling because they could not be provided with everything they wished from the commissariat. I heard one officer remark that not one of the European prisoners looked worth half a million of money. Each would cost about that sum for his release when the expenses of the war were calculated....

At Headquarters I found most of the foreign officers who had been sent by their governments to report on the operations. Among them was

Count Seckendorff,[5-12] whom I met here for the first time. He was on the suite of the Crown Princess of Prussia—our Princess Royal, afterwards the Empress Frederick. My name was not unknown to him, and as he was fond of drawing we became friends. Prince Edward had given me a letter of introduction to Lord Charles Hamilton,* brother to the Duke of Hamilton, who was one of Sir Robert's A.D.C.'s. The Headquarters mess, with these foreign officers, was a wonderful babel of tongues.

Captain Speedy* turned up here again. After I saw him at Peshawur he had left the service and gone to Abyssinia, remaining there about two years. Seeing, however, that nothing was to be made of Theodore or his country, he had managed somehow to leave, and had gone to New Zealand or Australia. When the war began, persons who could speak Abyssinian were scarce, and Speedy was telegraphed for, and attached to Headquarters as interpreter. H. M. Stanley was also in this expedition as correspondent of the *New York Herald*.[5-13]

As the troops had advanced, luggage had been left behind, and at the front they were all existing on the scantiest of means. Tents, mess dishes, and everything that could be spared had been dropped. There was a recognised deficiency of all comforts; no beer could be had at the front, and even rum was scarce; and each tent had to hold as many at night as the space would allow. As we marched back again the things left behind were picked up.

[With] Mr. Hormuzd Rassam, whose detention as a prisoner by Theodore, was the principal cause of the war, I began a friendship which has continued till the present day. He had charge of the Queen and her son [Alamayou], Theodore's only legitimate child.[5-14]

....The Queen was to have sat to me, but day by day the sitting was put off, as she was not well, and her death took place, so I never saw her. (*Autobiography*, 191–193)

21 April, Tues. Dalanta Plain. This morning the Released Prisoners left the Headquarters camp at about 8 o'clock, and about midday the Second brigade of the 1st. Division under Gen. Staveley* started on a small march to reach the cliff of the Jedda descent, which they would pass the next day. And thus begins the triumphal return from Victory.

Note: It is curious that Simpson omits any mention of a major event which took place on the afternoon of 20 April and all day on 21 April. This was the public auction of any loot held by any army personnel, with the resulting funds being distributed to the lower ranks. To quote Henry M. Stanley,

On the third day of our stay in our cantonment upon Dahonte Dalanta plateau, the articles for sale were ready for the auctioneer.

The roll of the drum assembled all the officers and crowds of on-lookers around the piled trophies of Magdala, which covered half an acre of ground.....Fathoms of finest carpets of all countries were spread about, and all the paraphernalia of a thousand churches glittered in the morning sunlight; and jostling each other in the characteristic confusion of mobs were the gentlemen buyers, who for the nonce were connoisseurs in antiquities, and displayed remarkable acumen in discerning tinsel from real, glitter from gold....

Bidders were not scarce. Every officer and civilian desired some souvenir of Magdala. One bought a cross of silver or brass, another a censer, another chose a sword. Goblets and cups, pyxes and chalices of silver, there were in plenty; silks, umbrellas, saddles resplendent with golden filigree, and starred with coloured stones; tents, carpets, richly illuminated Bibles and manuscripts, trinkets, and jewellery [all] found ready purchasers. Mr. Holmes, as the worthy representative of the British Museum, was in his glory. Armed with ample funds, he outdid all in most things; but Colonel Fraser* ran him hard because he was buying for a wealthy regimental mess—11th Hussars—and when anything belonging personally to Theodore was offered for sale, there were private gentlemen who outbid both.

When Theodore's shield, used by him in his younger days, was offered for sale, though only garnished by a few silver plates, the bidding became very energetic, and from ten dollars it speedily went up to 200 dollars, for which sum it was purchased by Colonel Fraser.

Mr. Holmes secured many interesting articles.

The auction lasted two days. The total receipts amounted to £5,000. This sum was divided among the non-commissioned officers and men who were southward of the Bashilo, which gave each man a trifle over four dollars.[5-15]

THE ORDER OF SOLOMON'S SEAL AND THE HOLY CROSS

This was an Order which Theodore wished to institute, so as to be able to confer honour on the British mission and upon one or two of his own principal chiefs.[5-16] There were to be three classes of the Order. And the insignia were made, but the misunderstanding which led to the imprisonment of our people occurred and the Order never was completed. The warrant for it was written and in Amharic, and translated into English by Mr. Rassam.

The Emblems are among the articles we found in Magdala, and are now in our Tosh Khana.[5-17] Those for the first class of the order are all in gold, same size as the sketch herewith sent. The second class are silver with gold cross in the centre; and the third class are all of silver.

The King intended to confer the first order upon Mr. Rassam, and upon his eldest son, Ras Mashaesha, also upon Ras Ingada, the chief Ras.[5-18] The second class of the order was intended for Dr. Blanc, Lieutenant Prideaux, Ras Tagga, Ras Wald Mariam, and Ras Gabrei.[5-19] The appointments to the third class of the Order never took place.

The double Triangle seems to be the symbol which is understood in Abyssinia as Solomon's Seal. Theodore's throne had three of them upon it; but the symbol which usually goes by that name is the five-pointed star. They are both Masonic emblems, and the power ascribed to these ancient symbols is very great. At first [these] emblems were in all probability symbolical of the Deity or of the Divine power, for one of the legends about Solomon's Seal is that it created the world. At a later period numbers got mixed up with these forms, such as we find in the Greek speculations, and the same powers were ascribed to them. Even the creation or origin of all things was said to be the result of the principle inherent in numbers.

A lower degradation was still in store for their ancient and sacred symbols. They became associated with astrology, and in this character they were the property, or stock in trade, of fortune tellers, magicians and tricksters of the legerdemain fraternity.[5-20]

The name of these emblems in Amharic, is *Nishan Ya Solomon Mahtam, Tanna Maskaloo*, and the title of the order would be similar, but without the word *Nishan,* which is equivalent to insignia. *Maskal* is the Amharic for cross.[5-21]

Priests and Villagers of Wadela Singing the Song of Moses Before Sir Robert Napier

†HE RE†URN Wi†H EXPEDi†iON FORCES

PART VI   Dalanta Plain to Lake Ashangi
22 April to 5 May

22 April, Wed. Dalanta Plain. The first brigade with the Commander-in-Chief and Staff moved to-day to the cliff of the Jedda. The queen of Theodore who is in camp was reported ill to-day and a Doctor was wanted.**6-1**

23 April, Thurs. Bethor. The whole Brigade started at 5 a.m. to cross the ravine or valley of the Jedda, and its steepness and difficulty may be understood when it is stated that it was 9 or 10 o'clock before everyone came in. Lord Charles Hamilton, A.D.C. to the Commander-in-Chief, who is suffering from a fall from his horse at Magdala, had to be brought in a dooley [covered litter] and he did not reach the camp at Bethor till half past nine at night, being the whole day in passing down and up the vast valley between the Dalanta and Wadela plains. All the tents and luggage were very late.

Sir Robert Napier was accommodated with a tent at the Station and while he was there waiting for the baggage to arrive, a large party of priests in their vestments with crosses, staffs etc., and a large ornamented red umbrella surmounted with a ball and a cross, approached to the tent and began singing the Song of Moses in the 15th Chapter of Exodus on the Horse and his rider—which they applied of course to Theodore.**6-2** They also sang a Psalm or rather a collection of extracts from the Psalms and other parts of the Old Testament. It began with "Oh Clap your hands you people and Shout with joy for the Deliverers have returned in peace;"**6-3** and they suited action to the word by clapping their hands. They certainly have great reason to be glad at the overthrow of their persecutor.

> On the morning when the Jedda had been passed on our return, and Sir Robert Napier had arrived, and was resting in a tent with a few of his staff, a large red umbrella made its appearance, along with a cross and other church properties. Then followed a number of priests with their large white turbans, and a vast concourse of people with the staffs used in psalm-singing, and the instrument like the ancient systrum....Their music is very wild and rude; to our ears it is anything but musical, and the

contrast of the while teeth with the dark skin when they open their mouths—which they do, very wide, in singing—produces a strange and by no means solemn impression. But here, under the circumstances, the most sceptical could not doubt their sincerity.

To them the death of Theodore must have been a most blessed release from a terrible fear; to them this Pharaoh had been a most hard task-master. To us, also, his conduct and fate had been like that of the true Pharaoh of Scripture. Long and repeatedly had he hardened his heart and refused to let the captives go, and it was only at last, under fear of terrible vengeance, that he allowed them to escape, and, like his prototype of old, their deliverance was soon followed by his own destruction. ("Jottings," 611)

24 April, Fri. Abdi coomb. We reached here this morning, a very short march, and we are now pushing on in regular order for the sea at Zoulla. Sir Robert had an interview with a number of the released native prisoners who got their liberty as a result of our expedition. One of them [was] Dajazmach Birroo Gosho, the Chief of Gojjam,[6-4] who had been long a prisoner of Theodorus. Sir Robert also gave an interview to the chief of Wadela whose plains we are now on.

25 April, Sat. Gahso. We came back on this march by a new route which a guide had declared to be a near cut, but somehow or other the guide went on in front and the head of the column could not tell in the number of paths which was the right one. This just occurred as Sir Robert Napier and his staff came up, and a halt was called. Aides de camp were sent to the point to find out the right road and others were sent to the rear to prevent the troops and baggage from going astray. After a halt of about fifteen or twenty minutes an officer returned announcing that the right path had been found, and we moved on. It is a very long march, even when shortened by a near cut. It was intensely cold in the morning and evening from the cold wind that blows on the top of the high plateau of Wadela.

26 April, Sun. Takazze. The cold so was great during the night that the water was frozen in the soldiers' tin dishes, and I saw a pool of water with ice upon it. We started early in our march. This morning the bugle sounded at 1/2 past four, and the start was to be five, and at that hour before the sun is up

RETURN OF THE ARMY FROM MAGDALA—THE MOUNTAIN TRAIN

the cold was intense and as we neared Santara, which is a gradual ascent, the wind increased and was very disagreeable.

The Santara camp had been moved down to the Takazze to await us there. Here all extra kit had been left on the advance upon Magdala, and to-day all are rejoicing at getting their additional tent accommodation and extra baggage. Rum has been once or twice served out to the camp and after such a long course of Total Abstinence it is looked upon as a very great treat. Tea and sugar are also beginning to be known again, their taste and quality having been almost forgot. The long absence of these ordinary necessities of life will indicate the hard lines every one has had to put up with in the advance upon Magdala. Although we now occasionally see such luxuries as rum, tea and sugar we are still very far from all danger of being pampered. To-day the Military Secretary and an officer in charge of a battery might have been seen, not only washing themselves in the Takazze, but also washing their flannel shirts, pocket handkerchiefs, towels, etc. Those who know what an Indian camp is will appreciate the idea of every man having their very own dhobie [washerman]. As yet all other servants are about equally scarce.

27 April, Mon. Takazze. From the length of the march yesterday and the difficulty of getting the baggage down the Ghaut of the Takazze, a portion of the things did not get in. Mules and their loads were arriving all through the night, and a few did not come down the ghaut till this morning. Owing to this long march we have halted here to-day. Yesterday Lieutenant Morgan* of the Royal Engineers died while being carried here in a dooley He had been ill for some time of fever and had been sinking for some days past.[6-5] To-day the funeral took place here in the burial ground of the church of Kydoos Gabriel,—or St. Gabriel,—with expressions of regret at the death of this young officer. I hear only of respect and admiration of his character. His illness is wholly attributed to his overwork of himself resulting from a desire to do more than his physical system was able to bear.

This church of St. Gabriel it would seem is a very old one, being at least seven or eight centuries since it was erected. There is a celebrated church about ten miles from this which is partly or wholly cut into the rock. It is the work of Lalibela [Lalibala],[6-6] a saintly king who reigned over all Abyssinia at that time; but before he got this church he built the church of Kydoos Gabriel, and used it until the more elaborate church which now retains his name was finished. Lalibala was of the family of Zagie [Zagwé], another son to the Queen of Sheba by another father than that of Menelik his brother.[6-7]

28 April, Tues. Muja. The march from the Takazze to Dildi is too long for one day, so it has been broken at this place, which is a little more than half way up to the Wandach pass.

On the way here I went into a church placed on the top of a conical hill with its grove of trees surrounding it. It is a round church, dedicated to St. Michael. There were only a very few people about the place. The priests were within the Sanctuary consecrating the Sacrament, and I managed, as the Beatalehem door was partly opened, to get a very slight glimpse of the ceremony.[6-8] The most important point that I observed was the administration of the sacrament by the priests to each other, after which the front door was opened and the Sacrament was brought to it, and although there was no one to receive it yet a long service was gone through, after which they retired and the door was shut. The consecrated bread was in what seemed a basket covered with a red and white cloth, almost the same as what I saw at Adigerat. And the priest while administering seemed as carefully to conceal it as I had noticed at that place. The wine was served with a spoon from the Chalice.

About a mile from Mashik there is a church. I went into it and although it was not seven o'clock there was no one in it: all had gone to their villages. This is the first round church that I have seen, and I understand that south from Antalo that they are all of that form. The necessity of keeping with the escort prevented me from making a plan of it. I may mention that it is like the square formed upon the plan of a three fold division and that the Sanctuary is square, the two outer courts only being round.

Theodore's Queen, who was ill with a bad cold from the bitter winds of the Plateau of Wadela, is again better, and is now expressing a wish to accompany her son to India, where he is to be sent as the best place suitable for his education.

> Immediately after her husband's death Robert Napier had written to her, on 14 April, about her son, and his future, saying, "It is to be feared that, in

the present state of Abyssinia, the youth's life will be in danger at the hands of many persons who will aspire to the empire of Abyssinia. We are willing to take the child under our protection, and send him to England or Bombay to be educated, and we would suggest this arrangement to you as the best that could be made. Your own wishes regarding his disposal shall, however, be followed by us." Houses of Parliament, *Further Papers*, 9.

The Queen had agreed to Napier's proposal. (Simpson in *The Illustrated London News:* published 27 June 1868)

29 April, Wed. Dildi. This is a heavy march. The descent from Wandach is long and in many places very steep and stony, making it hard work for man and beast to get along. In the descent one passes through more than one zone of vegetation. On the top of the pass the trees are small, but as you descend larger kinds appear, and at the stream, the Telharé River, the foliage is large and fine. The *Ficus* genera is to be found plentiful, and the Babob[6-9] with its rich and rather strong and heavy scent is in ample profusion on the lower half of the way. Mistletoe, a kind almost the same as we have it at home, is in thick clusters on the trees near the Telharé.

We found all the Elephants here.[6-10] They carry back the mortars and heavy guns, and from having to undergo the same hardships of want of proper and sufficient food which all have had to submit to, they are getting weak and unfit for the heavy burdens and hard roads which must tell at last on the strongest frames, and even Elephants, the most powerful of all the animal creation, are suffering and threatening to give up. We are to rest here for a day for the good of the Elephants and the other animals of the expedition, and it will not be unwelcome to the rest of the camp.

To-day I was surprised at an Abyssinian coming up to me and speaking English. He told me he had been in England and had come out as a colporteur [missionary] to distribute Bibles printed in the Amharic. The Bible is here always written on sheepskin, and a copy costs about 80 [Maria Theresa] dollars, while a printed copy can be supplied for about 4 Dollars, but I understand the Abyssinians don't care for the printed copies. They prefer the ancient written Bibles and Psalm books and those in the Geez [Ge'ez] language are such, although they do not understand the words in which it is written.[6-11]

RETURN OF THE ARMY FROM MAGDALA—THE ELEPHANT TRAIN

On Ethiopian manuscripts, Simpson later observed:

The books in Abyssinia are all written upon parchment, and their Bibles, Gospels, Psalms, &c., are all in the Geez or ancient Ethiopian, which, like the Latin, is now a dead language. But the antiquity which this implies maintains a strong claim on their veneration. Bibles and Testaments printed on paper have been sent out by the missionary societies, but the people of Abyssinia never took to them; the laboriously-written copies on sheepskin have a sanctity in their eyes which printed books can never acquire.("Jottings," 612)

[Simpson returns to his unexpected English-speaking visitor:]

This man was seized by Theodore and was imprisoned eight years at Debra Tabor. [6-12] He had only been a week or so at Magdala before our Expedition arrived, and to which he owes his freedom. His name is Mahdara Kal, and he is now employed as interpreter on the Staff of Colonel Phayre.*

The whole of the prisoners are one march ahead of us with the Second Brigade under Sir Charles Staveley. Mr. Rassam remains with the headquarters Staff, and has Theodore's Queen and young son to look after. She is now recovered from her late illness.

Mrs. Flad has excited a great deal of sympathy by adding one to the already numerous body of camp followers: in the shape of a Daughter. This took place at Gazu [Gahso] on the line of march. Mother and baby are both reported to be doing well.[6-13]

There is a report just come in that there has been a battle between Kasai of Tigray [Kasa of Tegray] and Gobzai of Lasta,[6-14] but its truth is very uncertain. Perhaps it is founded on belief that they are intending to have [a] struggle for the supremacy in Abyssinia. If they are to enter into this contest it will cause a great deal of disorder in the country. There was also a report, which was current among the Abyssinians, that the Egyptians have been moving upon Gondar, and that there had been fighting, but we have had no confirmation of it. If there is any truth in this it might give us some bother, but the doings between Kasa and Gobzai may go on, and we will not interfere.

One of the prisoners of Theodore, Faris Aly [6-15] that we released, being a man of note among the Abyssinians, started against another chief named Meshasha, son of Dajazmach Tadla, chief of Lasta, and uncle of Gobzai.[6-16] Faris Aly was not very successful in his attack and returned to the Yejoo country,[6-17] to which Meshasha followed him, where by the desertion of the most of his own soldiers he was made prisoner, and is now in the hands of Faris Aly, who by this stoke of fortune is already a long way on the road to dominion and power. These facts, or rather rumours, tell pretty clearly what the state of the country is likely to be for some time.

30 April, Thurs. Dildi. This morning it began to rain about 6 o'clock and came down heavily for about an hour and then began to clear up. The 49th had just started to march to Marawar when the rain came down, and the Elephants with the Armstrong Guns and Mortars had also to begin their march under the same circumstances.

1 May, Fri. Marawar. It again rained this morning, and in consequence the hour of marching was delayed. The tents were quite wet, and could not be dried before the start which added considerably to the loads for the baggage animals.

...I went over to Mr. Rassam's tent and sketched the boy. He was then seven years of age. He came into the tent dressed and with a shanah over all—that is, the white sheet with a broad red stripe near one of its edges—a necklace, and the matab, or blue cord of his baptism. The finishing touch, according to Abyssinian ideas of the toilet, had been given to him, by putting some butter or grease on his head. A small stream of it was trickling down the side of his face.

DAJAZMACH ALAMAYOU, SON OF THEODORE, LATE KING OF ABYSSINIA

A remarkable thing chanced with the reproduction of this portrait. When
it appeared in the *Illustrated London News,* it was really slightly more like
the boy than my picture, from which it was copied. The published
likeness is thus particularly good. This, of course, was an accident, but a
curious one. (Autobiography, 193)

On the way this morning I met my new acquaintance Mahdara Kal, which
name I am told means "The Habitation of the Word." There were some
Abyssinians with him, and one caught my eye from the peculiarity of his
costume. He wore a comb and a leather shirt, and in his hand was a basket
with some grain for his food, and a water bottle; he also carried a long stick
such as they use in the churches, the top of it was carved and ornamented
with crosses. I asked Mahdara Kal who he was, and the history I received is
I think worth relating.

The man had been at one time a Soldier of Theodore's, but like many more
he deserted. The King upon this seized his wife and two children, and burnt
them to death—This was his method of punishing deserters, and he has been
known to put twenty or thirty women and children into a house, shut the
door, and then set fire to it—When this man heard what had taken place it
so affected his mind that he determined to renounce the world and become
a monk, which he had done, and the dress which he wore was that of the
Order he had joined. He was now on his way to Zoulla with the troops, on
a pilgrimage to Jerusalem to visit the Holy Sepulchre,[6-18] and he is in hopes
of getting a passage to Suez.

Mahdara Kal also informed me that in the consecration of the Bread and
Blood, as he called it, that the Service is divided into chapters, and that at the
end of each chapter, the priests go round the *Tabot* three times, with a Cross,
incense and lighted candle. He did not confirm what I had heard about dancing
round the Tabot.

*Simpson later reverts to his encounter with the would-be visitor to Jerusalem
in his "Artist's Jottings." Describing Ethiopian monks, as well as the violence
of Téwodros, he observes:*

The monks wear a long robe or cloak of leather and a cowl, this last being their distinguishing mark, and "to take the cowl" is equivalent to saying that a man has become a monk. I met one of them during our morning march, and his strange outfit at once caught my eye. In addition to the leather dress and the cowl, he carried a small basket and a long staff with a cross carved on the top of it. While wondering what the man might be, for he had come along some distance talking to my Abyssinian servant, luckily I met one of our interpreters, who at my request interrogated him. He turned out to have been a soldier of Theodore's, but, like many more, towards the end of the king's career had deserted from the service.

Although he managed to escape himself, he had not been able to take with him his wife and two children. These Theodore made prisoners, and, according to his custom, placed them with the wives and children of other soldiers who had deserted, in a house, and then closing up the doors, set fire to it, roasting them alive. When the poor man learned their horrible fate, he renounced the world and "took the cowl." He was making his way with the army to Zoulla, in hopes of being able there to get a passage to Suez, and thus find his way to Jerusalem, so that he might visit the Holy Sepulchre, and there spend his life in service at the shrine. His worldly goods were comprised in a very small stock of food in the basket. He had a mild, good-natured expression about his face which predisposed me in his favour. ("Jottings," 610)

Reflecting in later life on such cruelty, Simpson discussed Téwodros' life and reign in his Autobiography, *where he wrote:*

A curious theory regarding Theodore occurred to me, which I have not seen suggested by any writer about the war. He was a wonderful man— another Napoleon, whether as great one cannot say. He had a more limited field of action than Napoleon; but he was able, had great mental power, ability, and ambition, and was at the same time bad and brutal. The cruelties related of him are terrible. Like Napoleon, he rose from almost nothing to be an Emperor. He had conquered the whole of Abyssinia; but an ambitious man is never satisfied, he always wishes to extend his power.

Now the Abyssinians have a prophecy that they will one day conquer Jerusalem, and that this will be achieved by them under a King named Theodore. This man, whose first name was Kasa, no doubt knew of that prophecy, and most probably adopted the name Theodore when he became Negoosa Negyst, with a view to fulfilling it. He likened himself to David, who from a shepherd boy became a monarch. If his previous history was like David's why not complete the whole likeness? David conquered Jerusalem, might not he do the same?

He could raise an army, but he had no artillery, and without artillery he felt himself powerless for such an undertaking.[6-19] The first question Theodore asked when any European arrived was, "Can you make guns?" If they said "No," he demanded, "Will you try to make guns?" If they refused to try, he kept them as prisoners in the hope that they would try. He did manage to have a big mortar made, and I think something in the shape of a gun or two had been attempted.[6-20] This intense desire for artillery tells in distinct language that he wished to extend his conquests beyond the boundaries of Abyssinia. Here, it seems to me, is the key to this man's conduct. It explains why he kept Europeans. Even if they could not make guns, he may have thought he could turn them to account in some way or another. This is only a guess on my part, but I believe it a suggestion which makes the whole of this man's conduct capable of being understood. (*Autobiography*, 198–199)

2 May, Sat. Marawar. Late last night a halt for a day had to be ordered. This was owing to the kit, or baggage, being still in great part behind on the line of march.

[Note: Simpson interviewed Hormuzd Rassam on this date, to provide additional background on Theodore and the origin of the conflict with Britain. Since this is covered in Rassam's own book, we have not included Simpson's notes.]

From Dildi to Marawar is a long march, said to be about 18 miles, but in addition to its great length, it is very hilly—no great ascent, but up and down all the way, and some of the places are very bad. It is a heavy march for one well mounted, and its difficulty to mules and pack animals heavily laden may be understood. Great numbers of mules broke down and died on the road, new animals had to be sent back for loading, and all the morning and forenoon men and loaded beasts, who had been out the whole night, might be seen toiling into camp weary and thoroughly done up. It was the afternoon as the rearguard came in, and they are supposed to be the last, it being their duty to see that no one is left behind.

About fifty mules are reported as being expended on this march. That with the time which it took some of them to come will convey perhaps a faint idea of the difficulties of moving troops and all the etceteras of a camp over such a country as this in a march of 800 miles over ground without roads, the mere tracks which have been formed by the constant passage of the native population. That is all that exists in the name of roads, and the tracks in these part of the country go over heights or descend into valleys to a depth or height equal to the highest mountains of Wales or Scotland.

When we start in the morning we see a mountain from our camp, which we know is as high as Snowden or Benaris, and we have to pass within a hundred feet or so of its summit and down the other side, carrying guns, tents, stores; and the sick who are unable to walk have to be carried over such a height. Everything necessary for a camp must be raised three or four thousand feet and got down again. By trying to conceive this operation, over a bad footpath, any one may form some estimate of the enormous difficulties an Expedition such as this has to contend with.

If the inhabitants of it [Abyssinia] had been against us the Expedition must have had to stop at once. All that we are bothered [with] is here and there a case of looting some solitary baggage. In the march of yesterday, or of yesterday and today, there seems to have been a good deal of stealing from stragglers.

A number of Abyssinian Prisoners were brought in this afternoon, and their cases were carefully gone into. Sir Robert Napier has in the most of these charges, where the evidence was conflicting, rather leant to mercy's side, but in this case it was very clearly made out against [them], and as many efforts of the same kind were reported as having occurred, an example was necessary and they were handed over to get 50 [lashes] each. It may illustrate the curious

Christianity of this country to state that the first of these men after he got his punishment he walked away with a stride, and said, referring to the fifty lashes he had received, "What was that to him who was the slave of Christ?"

To be indifferent to a crime of stealing, and to the effects of fifty lashes on the bare back, is a high state to have arrived at. Those Advanced Christians at home who have got beyond the Ten Commandments ought to note that their Abyssinian brethren are also in the same advanced state. Theodorus himself being a most illustrious example, not one of the ten words but he has violated, and that too repeatedly. The Military Authorities have not yet reached this advanced stage, and seem as if they intended to produce a slight deference for the command that "Thou shalt not steal."

To-day the same rumours about the battle between Kasa and Gobzai, including the death of the latter, and the advance of the Turks upon Gondar have been repeated but not believed.

3 May, Sun. Lat. Comparatively with the march from Dildi this is a short one, but it is quite long enough. The usual march in India is about 12 miles, but that is along a level road. The march to-day was nearly all up hill, and a slight descent to the camping ground, which was moved from its old position to avoid the smell of dead mules and other effluvia peculiar to camps. A good rattling of thunder went in after midday and a little rain fell.

4 May, Mon. Mussagita. This camp also goes by the name of Wofela or Offala. Wofela is the name of the large plain upon which the camp is pitched, and Mussagita is the name of a considerable village on a hill overlooking the plain, hence the two names. The march to-day was an easy one, an ascent from Lat, and a descent to this extended plain. On the top of the pass the wild rose bush might be seen of a size to justify the name of Rose Tree for the most of them were at least twenty feet in height and they were in full bloom, covered with large white flowers. The only difference between them and the white dog rose of the hedges of England is that the former are slightly larger than the latter. Mixed in masses with this white rose is a St. John's Wort—*Hypericum*[6-21]—which grows about the same height, and its yellow flowers are about as large as the flowers of the other. They are in rich, thick clusters and the two growing together produces a very beautiful effect.

About half way down towards the plain of Wofela there is a church in a group of trees of the juniper cedar kind. It is dedicated to the Saviour, as Medhanie Alam [Medaarne Alum?] or "The Medicine of the World." On the way near the church I saw a bag of bones but took no notice of them, and at the door of one of the outhouses I found another bag. The bag was of leather and it contained human remains. This was evident from the skull. These offerances looked as if the place had been deserted, but I had just met the priests coming from the church, and they had asked me whether I was a Christian—their usual question—and when I got to the church the scent of incense was still perceptible, so that I cannot account how the bones, of what I have no doubt were those of saints, were left in such a position.

Although an easy march it was evening ere the rear guard got in, and they reported an attack by the Abyssinians on the way, and that they had fired thirty rounds of Snider into them. This order to fire has been the result of constant efforts to loot the rear guard and stragglers.

5 May, Tues. Lake Ashangi. Rain in the morning seems to be a daily event. Luckily to-day it did not last long. In the afternoon rockets and shells were fired into the lake. It was done by way of experiment and it got rid of some useless weight which has to be carried. Quantities of ammunition have been destroyed at Wofela and Dildi to save carriage. A raft was made to-day and the lake was sounded. It was found to be 102 feet in depth. An effort was made to discover if there were any fish but none could be got. Otters were reported, and if this is correct it would lead to the supposition that there must be fish somewhere. Duck and geese are in large quantities in the water. The latter has no visible outlet. General Malcolm C.B., who was at Antalo when I passed that place, came to Wofela yesterday, and leaves tomorrow for Antalo again.

Count Kielmansegge of the Austrian navy, the companion of Captain Kodolitsch, who had to remain behind sick, is again well and has joined the Head Quarters.

There is report of a new Abuna having been appointed. This is always done by the Coptic Patriarch at Cairo when an Abuna is wanted. A messenger has been [to be?] sent with 800 [Maria Theresa] dollars, 400 of which is for the patriarch, and the other 400 for the new Abuna. **6-22** It is also said that the new Abuna has gone to Gobzai, if so that will give him an advantage in the race for the Emperorship, because the ceremony of investiture to such a rank can only be performed by the Abuna; and as all the priests of Abyssinia must receive their induction from the head of the church, the possession of such a high functionary by one of the powers here is a great political triumph.

Expanding on the report of the arrival of a new Abuna, Simpson later wrote:

Since the death of the last Abuna there has been no new appointment. When we returned from Magdala we heard a rumour that a successor was on his way to Abyssinia, and that he was to take up his residence in Gobzai's territory, but no doubt this was only one of the many rumours afloat about the expected struggle for power that was naturally to be looked for after the death of Theodore. Should a new one be sent, the possession of him for political ends will excite the whole of the country. He is consecrated by the Patriarch of the Egyptian Coptic Church, and eight hundred [Maria Theresa] dollars have to be paid for the purpose; four hundred for the ceremonies of consecration, and four hundred for the expense of the Abuna's journey to Abyssinia. Whoever can secure the next one, will be in the best position for succeeding Theodore as the *Negus Negyst,* or "King of kings."**6-23**

The Abuna is the head of the Abyssinian branch of the Coptic Church. He is the only Bishop; no one in Abyssinia holds a similar rank. The appointment of all the clergy is made by him. The only other church functionary of importance is the head of the monks. He is called the *Itchegé* [Echagé]. His relations to the Abuna I cannot define, but he has the appointment of the heads of all the monasteries, and the control over their government. ("Jottings," 610)

There was an old man in our camp who possesses the title of Emperor, and is said to claim that he is of the legitimate descent of the ancient Emperors, and I suppose can trace his blood back to Menelik.**6-24** It is the custom of those who by their energy rise to power to keep one of this family—for I learn that there are a good many of them in existence with the same descent—as a puppet, a practice not unknown in other parts of the world. This man is called *Hadsie Johannis,* which means the Emperor John.**6-25** *Hadsie* is a title that can only be used by an Emperor with the blood descent. Theodore was not called Hadsie. He used the title Negoosa Negyst, "King of Kings." He also used the most ancient of all titles for Emperor in the country, which is *Jan*, but it may be said to be now obsolete, unless in a sort of innovative form as *Jan Hoy!* or "Oh Jan!"[6-26] It is said that it was from this word that the legend of Prester John was supposed to belong to Abyssinia.[6-27]

Theodore would not condescend to have one of the Hadsie family as a corner to his power, but had himself, and I think he was the first man who tried this independent action in this country, crowned as Emperor of Abyssinia.

Hadsie Yohannis is said to have the full power of making chiefs as nobles, and [it is reported] that he would be most willing to give anyone the title of *Ras* for thirty dollars. As I was told that I could get such an honour at so low a figure, I was almost inclined to invest, for it must be one of the most ancient titular distinctions. It is the root of the first word in the Hebrew Scriptures— Berasit, *in principio,* the Head or fountain from which all creation spring by the Divine Will. With such an ancient handle to your name, one need not be ashamed to appear at any court of Europe, and for such a privilege thirty dollars is dirt cheap.

Reverting to the puppet 'Emperor' Yohannes, and his power to nominate people up to the rank of Ras, Simpson later observed:

The old legend of Prester John belonging to Abyssinia seems to have arisen from the ancient name of the king, which was *Jan.* This word is not used now except in the invocation form; "*Jan-Hoi!*" being used for "O King!" There are many in Abyssinia who claim a blood descent from the ancient kings, and they have the title of *Hadsie.* One of these was found as a prisoner in Magdala, and bore a sort of double title of *Hadsie Johannes.* He was a very old man, weak in body, and almost imbecile in mind; but he had, in virtue of this blood descent, the power of bestowing rank, and it was said that he would make any one a *Ras* for thirty dollars. There is not a more ancient title in any court of Europe, and only think of securing such a distinction for thirty dollars, and at the hands, too, of a lineal descendant of Prester John. ("Jottings," 613)

PART VII: LAKE ASHANGI TO ANTALO
6 May to 12 May

6 May, Wed. Haiya. This is a short march—said to be only about 8 miles—and we thought it would be an easy one, but the saddle of a range of hills had to be got over, and the narrowness of the road caused a good many stoppages, from mules falling, and every stoppage arrests the whole column.

A storm was brewing overhead the most of the day which at last burst over us in the afternoon deluging the whole camp with rain. A few preliminary drops which came down made the road so bad that the last of the baggage had a hard job to get in. The narrow road got so slippery that the mules stumbled and fell at every step. It was nine or ten o'clock at night before the rear guard got into camp and reported that the last man and beast had arrived—by that time the ground was like a marsh, flash after flash of lightning blazed around in the camp making the candle light in the tents seem darkness, and the thunder roared seemingly in the very midst of us. By digging trenches round the tents some escaped a little of the flood of rain that followed. As for the numerous camp followers who got their fires put out and had no tents or covering, I cannot say how they managed. The most ardent thirst for knowledge must have been instantly extinguished, had an effort been made to go out in such a night. But I must say it is really wonderful how the natives of Hindustan can manage to get through a night such as we have just had.

The camp was pitched at this place which is about 4 or 5 miles from Makan, the next station, so as to divide the march into two. It is a very beautiful locality, the tents are pitched in green terraces and are surrounded with trees, principally of the juniper cedar.[7-1] A fine wooded valley runs up behind the camp, which terminates in some grand craggy peaks which overlook lake Ashangi. Probably it was to these very high peaks that we were mainly indebted for those thorough drenching that we got last night.

The woods on the mountains are very full of a plant that has been much noticed by African travellers, that is the *Erica Arborea Giganta Africana,* or African Gigantic Heath.[7-2] It may be seen here from a few feet in height growing as high as twenty feet. It is a very light, elegant tree with a large quantity of small flowers of a whitish colour.

7 May, Thurs. Makan. This was a very short march, not above five miles. Owing to the rain of the night before the hour of marching was changed to 10 o'clock. This gave the tents and everything a little time to get dry in the sun, and it also allowed the road a little time to get firm. This is the place where there is such a beautiful country, of fine fields but no cultivation, all is left desolate. I learn that the locality is called "the hunting ground of the Gallas," and that will sufficiently explain the appearance of the country, the "hunting" of the Gallas being after the cattle, sheep and other property of the inhabitants, and this lucrative sport is carried on by burning the villages and murdering and mutilating the persons of the[ir] rightful property.

I hear that there is in Abyssinia, and [this] extends to a great many places in Africa, an ancient system of assurance for the loss of property, by plunder or otherwise. If a man is plundered, everyone in the locality makes him a present until something equal to the amount of his loss is made up. This is a custom so long and so faithfully kept up that it realises all the benefits of an Assurance Company. But it even goes farther, for on all marriages, presents of cattle, sheep, mules and everything necessary to set up the young couple, are made by the neighbours.

8 May, Fri. Bulago. A large portion of the Brigade has been separated and sent on in advance. This had become necessary because every station we pass, whatever troops might be at them, is absorbed into our column, so that we have been like a rolling snow ball, increasing as we move along, until we had become far too large. The officer of the rear guard on the march from Ashangi, reports that for six hours there was a constant flow of life which kept pouring out along the line of march. As we start about 6 o'clock in the morning this would make it midday before the last of the column left the camp, which is far too late. At Antalo the first Division, which has been marching on its return from Magdala in two Brigades, will be divided into five, and in that form will return to Senafe and Zoulla.

This was a short march, but there was a very bad bit to ascend before reaching the camp. Another deluge of rain to-night which made a swamp of the whole place, and made a very uncomfortable night for the most of the men.[7-3]

9 May, Sat. Attala. Owing to the downfall of rain making the roads bad and the tents heavy, the start was delayed till 10 o'clock. It began by a steep ascent up to the saddle of the Fera mountain, then a deep descent to the plain of Ayba. Out of this plain there is a very slight rise to the Kesad Bota, or saddle of Bota, and then over the other side is a long and steep zig-zag down to Attala.

There was a little rain to-night, but after last night it was as nothing. The question as to when the rains will come on has many different opinions upon it. According to some they begin about the middle of May, with occasional showers, and become permanent in June. But our best authority declares that May is a dry month, and that the present storms are nothing, and that the rains do not begin till the middle of June. If this is the case the army will be easily got out of the country before the wet season comes on. [7-4]

10 May, Sun. Mashik. This march is over the pass on the east side of Mount Alajá where Walda Yasous has an *Amba* or fort.[7-5] We could see, when we reached the top of the pass, the houses stuck in the crevices of the rock, like eagles' nests. The perpendicular rock must render each place perfectly impregnable. How the siege or the defence of such [a] stronghold is carried on is quite beyond all my ideas of military engineering; or how any living being except an eagle or a hawk could have thought of existing in such a place, and at such a height, upwards of 10000 feet high, is equally beyond my powers of conception. Such forts are pretty good indications of the state of the country, and the relations existing between the chiefs.

Walda Yasous, or the Son of Jesus, is the chief of Wogara,[7-6] and as he is placed exactly between Kasa of Tegray and Gobzai of Lasta, both of whom want to subdue him, he has a difficult game to play. Kasa had an army out a few weeks ago for the purpose of bringing him into subjection, but it has now gone off in another direction, I suppose with more important business to occupy it.

On getting over the last pass we leave behind us all the difficult country. The two marches into Antalo are very easy and all after that to Zoulla is a good well made road. To-day news came up that a very heavy fall of rain has damaged the Sooroo pass. Although some parts of the road have suffered severely, it will soon be put to rights again and be in perfect order for the troops to pass.[7-7]

11 May, Mon. Masgeh. This morning on starting on the march I heard the firing of a funeral party. I learned that it was a corporal, of the name of Haris, of the 4th King's Own, who had died of dysentery. I passed the poor fellow on the march of yesterday, and it was evident that he was beyond all hope. It is worth remembering that such cases exist, even on a Return from Victory. We have a dark side to our picture. While the mass of the force are glad that the war is over, flushed with success, and delighted at returning home again, there is a long string of doolies to be seen on the line of march each with its inmate either sick, or those who were wounded at Magdala. Roberts, who was struck in the arm at Arogee,[7-8] has had to have the limb amputated to-day. These are the shadows which belong to an existence such as this.

It will also assist in giving an idea of the wants of such an Expedition by stating that when I passed yesterday the poor fellow who [later] died, there were at least eight dooley bearers, a native medical officer, with attendants to carry water, medicines, and medical comforts, and there were one if not two of the 4th as a guard. More or less such are the requirements of each sick man. From this an idea may be formed of what would have been the trouble and labour if there had been long and continual fighting at Magdala, with its necessary results of wounded men.

A number of monks came down from a monastery in the hills with offerings of citrons and other fruits. A gentleman who had visited their monastery reported that they had complained to him about a Galla chief who, when the Camp had passed before, was fed for some days and got a present in dollars when he left. Such was the way a "heathen" had been treated, while they who were "Christians" had not received any of these kind attentions. General Merewether* had heard of this before they came to him with their offerings of fruit, and he would not receive them nor their presents for being guilty of such falsehoods, for he states that they were fed for some days and got a present of money. Their monastery is a very small place. It was founded by Abba Kathala, at present it has only an Acting head who is the Abba till another is appointed. This man's name is Gebra Tsion or "The Slave of Zion." He was one of the deputation to-day and wore a white turban and a yellowish leather cloak, with crosses painted upon the bands with which it [was] fixed across his breast.

I am told that the ground[s] of the monasteries in Abyssinia are all well cultivated by the monks. They grow lots of vegetables and fruits. There is at a place called Waldubba, in the north-west, a valley containing monks and nuns to the extent of fifteenth thousand, and it is all beautifully cultivated by them.7-9

There is only one order of monks in Abyssinia. They are dedicated to St. Antonius. There is a Head over the whole order who is the Idjégé 7-10

12 May, Tues. Antalo. On the march this morning we met Brigadier General Llorante and Lieutenant Colonel the Comte de Mirasol, two Spanish officers who have arrived to see and report to their government respecting the mode in which the war is being carried on in Abyssinia. 7-11

> One remarkable feature of this Expedition was that almost every Government in Europe sent officers with it to report upon its organisation. The Indian troops were no doubt an attraction for foreign Governments to learn something about. France, Austria, Prussia, and even Holland and Spain sent officers. I think two for each country were allowed to proceed.
>
> The two Spanish officers came late. One was an old General, who was anxious about comforts, and he was reported to have inquired of some one when he arrived at Zoulla as to which was the best hotel in Antalo. The name of that place, for some reason or another, was in large letters on the map, so he thought it would be an important town. This was passed on as a good joke, for he might as well have expected hotels in the centre of Africa. Antalo was some distance from our camp, but I should say from its appearance that it had about a dozen houses, formed of wattle and daub, with thatched roofs. (*Autobiography*, 188)

As the whole force is now to move in five columns, we will halt here till the fifteenth in order to let the other columns move on in advance. The Head Quarters will move with the fifth and last. Antalo is 15 marches from Zoulla, but some of the regiments may have to stop at Senafe till the ships are perfectly ready for them to embark on their arrival at Zoulla.

Another birth is reported among the released prisoners.

13 May, Wed. Antalo. Colonel Milward* is to proceed home with official dispatches of the Capture of Magdala. He is also to take home the triple crowned mitre of the Abuna. It has been tested and is found to be solid gold all over. The prize committee have valued it at £2000, and it has been claimed by them, and it is to realise its true value that it is to be sent to England.[7-12] As the crown had in the first place been secured by Mr. Holmes for the British Museum,[7-13] no doubt but they will get the first offer of it. The Chalice, of which a drawing was sent, has also been tested and is of solid gold. Sir Robert Napier has also sent a royal robe which belonged to Theodore, and his royal seal, a drawing of which is here sent[7-14]—as presents to the Queen.

14 May, Thurs. Antalo. Another day's rest.

15 May, Fri. Antalo. As the church at Chelicut is celebrated as one of the best in this part of the world, a party was formed to visit it on the march this morning, and an escort of the 3rd Dragoon guards were sent with us. Chelicut is a large village, or perhaps in Abyssinia it might be called a town.[7-15] The houses have nice gardens and trees about them. There is a mixture of houses, some built square and others round.

At the east end in the midst of a grove of very fine large trees stands the church.[7-16] It is the largest and finest I have yet seen. Some of the doors or screens are ornamented with carving, and the interior is elaborately painted with scripture subjects, and the sufferings of saints. From the sacristy they produced a large number of very rich vestments, including two priestly crowns. I cannot call them mitres for they were not of that shape. They were like the dome of a church surmounted by a cross. They also produced a golden ring with the British arms upon it, which had been given them as a present by some of our envoys.[7-17]

When I was leaving the place my Abyssinian attendant beckoned me into a house close to the church. Here I found a little stout man with a very large turban, beside whom I was requested to sit. I was told that he was the *Alika* and one of the priests used the word "Episcopus," but I believe that "Rector" is nearer the dignity of his position.[7-18] Having some rum in my flask I offered the Alika a drop which he accepted, and a younger functionary held up a cloth to veil the operation of drinking,[7-19] but after he had imbibed he seemed to express his satisfaction with the liquor. I then poured out a little and holding it up, by means of the word "Salaam" which is truly a word for health.[7-20] I drank the health of the Episcopus and his brethren of the church of Chelicut.

One of them had a cross in his hand and about half an hour before when he was asked its price he held up all the fingers of his hands to express the number of dollars. It was now offered to me for three, and accepted.

By using the words "Beata Episcopus" which was the utmost extent that my knowledge of Amharic could take me, I learnt that I was in the Bishop's House.[7-21] It seemed like a court leading to a stable. There was a good deal of straw about, and the Episcopus sat on [a] built bench with a few skins below him. There is an inscription in Amharic on the cross I bought which is characteristic of the religious feelings of the country. It is "This cross belonging to Welata Tzion"—(the Daughter of Zion)—who has given it to Tzim (a church [or person] of that name) in the hope it may be to her a guide to Heaven."

Referring to the above visit to the cleric, in his "Artist's Jottings" Simpson later wrote:

Chelicut was the finest church that we saw on our line of march; it was less of a barn and more of a house than the others. There was some carving in wood which the priests pointed out to us with pride, and their vestments were much more elaborate than any that we had seen. They made a great display of their ecclesiastical property, which they turned out for the inspection of our party when I visited this church.

When leaving the place I was invited into a house near the church, which turned out to be that of the chief priest. I found him seated on a raised bench of earth, in what would be called the hall or court of a European house. It was littered about with straw, odds and ends, like a place for horses or cattle. Not knowing that I was in the episcopal palace, I begun to inquire who the principal figure was among those present, when one of the men, pointing to the priest seated on the bench, pronounced the word "Episcopus." On turning to salute this important personage, who was a very little man with a very large turban, he invited me to a seat upon the episcopal bench, which I at once accepted. In return for this honour I at once produced a flask of rum, and managed, more by signs than by words, to discover that his lordship was quite prepared for any amount of that sort of thing; so I filled out a good allowance in a cup for him. I cannot describe how he imbibed it, for one of the boys, or deacons, came forward with a sheet, of which he made a screen, and concealed the whole process. I can only say that I heard sounds of sipping and sucking, as if, instead of disposing of the rum at one gulp, he was extending the pleasure as far as he could.

When this veiled prophet became again visible, I filled up my cup, and by means of the word "salaam," and, "looking towards" them, managed to get them to understand that I was drinking their health. As they used the word "Ingleese," I think they comprehended that such was the English custom, which must have seemed as odd in their eyes as the bishop's manner did in mine. I was only sorry that my ration of rum would not permit of giving them a taste all round. Still, the good fellowship manifested produced its effects, for a cross was offered to me for three dollars, for which ten had been asked of our party not long before in the church. It is a comparatively small one, about eleven inches in length, and is similar to those used by the priests in reading the service, and for presenting to the congregation to kiss. This cross contains, engraved in Amharic, a very pretty inscription—"Cross belonging to Walata Tsion" (the daughter of Zion); "having been given by her to Tsion" (some church of that name), "that it may become to her a guide to the Heavens."

As there is only one bishop in Abyssinia, the Abuna, I think that my rum-sucking friend is not entitled to that rank. "Episcopus" was, perhaps, the only word that we mutually understood, and so it was used.

I think I was indebted for the honour of invitation to the house from a message having been sent with my Abyssinian servant, telling the priests to come over to the camp and get a few of the books that were found in Magdala. About 900 volumes were in that place when the expedition arrived, and Sir Robert Napier considered that it would be wrong, particularly in a country where books are so scarce, to take so many copies of the Scriptures away. Hence, after copies had been selected for the different libraries of India and England, as well as the principal libraries of Europe, he determined to distribute the remainder among the various churches on the line of march. It was also known that these books found in Magdala had been plundered by Theodore from the churches of the different provinces which he had conquered, and so it was, to a certain extent, as if we were returning them again to their rightful owners.[7-22] Chelicut being an important place, a good number of books were presented to the church. (*Jottings*, 612)

PART VIII: ANTALO TO SENAFE - May 16 to May 24

16 May, Sat. Dolo. Last night the Queen or rather Empress died and this morning the march was stopped from 6 till 10 o'clock on account of the funeral.[8-1]

Looking back on the great storm they had witnessed, and the ensuing day of mourning, for the queen, Simpson later wrote:

That evening at Eikhullet there was a terrible storm of thunder and rain. We were at such an altitude on the tableland, the thunder did not seem to be in the clouds above us, but we were in the thunder. The crashing peals sounded as if only outside our tents. The rain poured, and in the midst of this outburst of nature news came that the Queen was dead. Messengers were sent off to Chelicut for the priests to come and perform the funeral services, and our early march in the morning was ordered to be postponed. When I got up next morning the Queen's tent had become a chapel, in which the priests, my friend the "Episcopus" among them, were chanting prayers beside the body.

The Queen's servants were wailing round the tent for the loss of their mistress. Her female attendants had put on her richly-embroidered mantles, or carried in their hands, which they held aloft, some article belonging to her, such as a slipper or scarf. One had her drinking-horn. While they waited they danced about in an uncouth manner. I learned from some one who understood the language that they were calling her by all the endearing terms which could express their attachment and grief at losing her. One particular name by which they called her was "Supper." I suppose they meant she was their food and support. Some of them did that which is forbidden in Scripture—they scratched their foreheads with their nails till the blood came.

At last a litter was prepared, and the funeral procession moved away to Chelicut. A richly-ornamented umbrella was borne before the body. The priests were around the litter chanting. One held up a large processional cross, another waved incense, and the attendants continued their strange antics. They had four or five miles to go, and I wondered whether they would be able to keep up the wail and the antics all that way. I understood that the body was to be deposited in the church of Chelicut. (*Autobiography*, 194–195.)

At the mourning for the Queen, the attendants, after the manner of the country, while waiting they scratched their foreheads and temples till the blood came. This custom must be very old, for it is prohibited by Moses, "Ye shall not make any cuttings in your flesh for the dead, nor print any marks upon you." Lev. 19:28.; "Ye are the children of the Lord God: ye shalt not cut yourselves, nor make any baldness between your eyes for the dead." Deut. 19:1. See also Jer. 16:6, 7.

Reverting once more to the Queen's funeral in his "Artist's Jottings," Simpson later wrote:

At the death of the queen of Theodore we had another illustration of their religious ceremonies. Tirroo-Wurk, or "Pure Gold," as she was called, was a daughter of the Prince of Oubie, and she had been induced to accept Theodore when a mere child, in the hope of effecting the release of her father, who had been a prisoner for a long period.

Marriage, according to the rites of the Church in Abyssinia, is performed by taking the sacrament together in church, and when this ceremony has been gone through the marriage is indissoluble. Like the Greek Church, they allow of no divorce, and strange to say, it is the women of Abyssinia who most strongly object to this binding form of marriage. They say that, when thus bound, if their husband should ill use them, they cannot leave him. From this has resulted a very loose code of ideas respecting the marriage state, and it is to this cause that we must attribute the greater part of that gross immorality which was so much talked about by the corespondents with the expedition. Theodore was no exception among his countrymen, but the daughter of Oubie was the only wife to whom he was legitimately married by the sacrament of the Church.

It is evident that she never loved him; many were the quarrels between them, and it is said that she was the only person in Abyssinia who was not afraid of that terrible and wonderful man. One day she omitted to rise

Funeral of the Widow of King Theodore at Ekullet

121

when the king entered her tent, and on his fiercely demanding the reason of this want of respect, she, reading the book of Psalms at the time, replied, "Because she was communing in the presence of a greater king than him." This was a severe stab at Theodore's feelings, for King David was his grand model. He carried about with him a copy of the Psalms for constant study; he imitated their style of language, and often quoted their words in relation to himself and his enemies. He also claimed a resemblance between himself and David in their fortunes; they had both been obscure, and had fought, almost as boys, against the enemies of their country; success had in each case followed their efforts, and both had risen to thrones. This was a favourite subject of conversation with Theodore, and no words could have been more cutting to his pride than those of the queen.

He never lived with her again. She was sent to Magdala, where she was kept in a sort of semi-imprisonment with her son for about six years, and was only released with the other prisoners when Magdala was taken by the expedition.[8-2]

At first, when the queen came with the army in its return, her purpose was to go back to her family in Semien.[8-3]Afterwards she declared her wish to go with her son to Bombay, and she was with our camp at the time when her death took place. It occurred at Aikullet, on the evening of the 15th of May, during a wild storm of thunder and rain. On a high table-land about seven thousand feet high, you are not beneath, but actually in the clouds, which are bursting around you like a deluge; the thunder did not appear to be above, but around us; bright, grand flashes of lightning made the inside as well as the outside of every tent lividly visible, and the rain beat loudly and ceaselessly on the canvas roof. It was under these circumstances, while the storm was at its height that the widowed queen closed her short and stormy life.

As the army had to march, the funeral was arranged for next morning. The priests from Chelicut were there early. They filled the tent where the body lay, and, so far as I could see, the service was performed the same as I had witnessed in church [on Palm Sunday]. The priests had their vestments on, the large cross was there, holy water, incense, &c. The only thing I noticed as peculiar to the occasion was a large brazier of burning ashes in the centre of the tent. The service seemed to be a succession of prayers and psalms, and it went on the whole morning till the body was removed.

Outside of the tent the queen's female attendants were going through another performance. Each of them had something belonging to their mistress, as her articles of dress, personal ornaments, slippers, drinking cup, &c.; with these in their hands, and held above their heads, they were wailing after the custom of the country, and they staggered about in a manner that rendered it quite uncertain whether it was meant as a dance or the result of intoxication. They mingled words of endearment with complaint at their loss of a mistress. They called her "mother" and "our supper." This last phrase I was told is one of the most endearing terms of the language; and possibly it may have arisen from the sacrament being called the "supper." They also said, "We do not deserve to live when God has taken away one so good."

For hours this excited state was kept up, and before the funeral took place they were tearing their hair, and rubbing and scratching their foreheads till the blood came. I saw them leave the camp with the procession, seemingly getting more excited as they went on. The band of the 4th Regiment (King's Own) played the Dead March in *Saul* as the funeral began to move; and a party of the men of the same regiment marched with it. The priests arranged themselves round the body, and still continued the service for the dead as they went along.

The burial took place in the church of Chelicut, about three miles distant from the camp. (*Jottings*, 611–612)

17 May, Sun. Agoola. There is no "latest news" now to send except it be that every man of the army is now within 12 marches of Zoulla. It is 4 marches from this to Adigerat, 3 more to Senafe, 5 to Zoulla, but by means of the railway it is said that a day can be saved.

18 May, Mon. Dongolo. There was one shop at our last camp and brandy was quoted at five dollars a bottle, or a little over twenty shillings. Even at that figure I saw not only a metaphorical run on the market, but the pedestrian act which that word expresses, by an individual who was anxious to secure some of this valuable liquor. Figs at seven [Maria Theresa] dollars a box are enough to bring in the name of the prophet in connection with their sale.

At this place there is a rock-cut church, and if our information regarding this is correct, it must be one of the oldest churches in Abyssinia.[8-4] It is said to have been excavated in the 4th century by two kings named Abraha, or "He who has brought the light," and Atsbaha, or "He who has brought the Dawn."[8-5]

According to Ludolf the first to introduce Christianity were "des Princes Abreha & Atzbeha."[8-6] Other authorities state that these were twin Kings who ruled in Abyssinia when Christianity was introduced.

19 May, Tues. Tsád Amba. To reduce the march of the morrow we passed Ad Abaga, and came about three miles further to this camping ground.

On the march to-day I went off the road to visit what seemed to be a very impressive looking village. It owed this character to a very high wall, and a large gateway, but within I found it to be a very poor place. The most important building in it was the place for the cows. It was of stone. The most of the houses were mere wigwams of straw, with an earthen bench for a bed, a pot or so, and a fire on the floor in the middle. I tried to get milk but failed in the effort. I do not think there was any in the place. It seemed comfortless and cheerless in the extreme.

20 May, Wed. Mai Wahiz. An officer of the 4th King's Own committed suicide by shooting himself in his tent. Drinking is said to have been the cause, D.T. [*delirium tremens*] the result, and temporary insanity the immediate cause of the act.

21 May, Thurs. Adigerat. This place is wonderfully improved since we passed it. The Transport lines are like a garden, [and] a well has been dug and planted with flowers all round. I called it a *Kooah* [?], but the Hindoo to whom I spoke looked dignified and called it a *Bowlee,* a term which is only applied to wells in India of a general architectural character.

22 May, Fri. Focada. This place is also very much improved. A long line of huts have come into existence. The Mule Hospital is also very much beautified. Sir Robert Napier and Staff went round and inspected everything when he arrived.

23 May, Sat. Goun-Gouna. We have lately heard that the Released Prisoners are not getting on very well. There is a difficulty in getting them to attend to camp regulations, and when they are told that orders must be carried out, they demand, "Are we Still Prisoners?" Many of them have expressed their regret that they were taken away from Magdala. It would seem that one or two individuals quietly slipped away from camp at Antalo, and went to Adowa and Aksum. Many were anxious to go, but Sir Robert did not think it prudent, and in his anxiety to get the army past the Sooroo pass he has given up all idea of visiting these places himself.[8-7]

One of the party has just joined us to-day, and I have heard his account of these two places. There is one obelisk standing at Aksum, another is fallen, and a few smaller stones are standing.[8-8] The large obelisk is about 20 or 30 feet high. At its bottom there is a representation of a door, and the tradition is that if it could be opened that it would lead into chambers of gold. There are inscriptions in Greek and Amharic on the obelisks and stones about the city.[8-9] Coins and pottery are always found in digging and often after the rains antiquities have been exposed by their influence.[8-10]

The old church at Aksum has been three times built.[8-11] A very large flight of stairs leads up to it. It is supposed to contain the Real Ark of Solomon's Temple. When Menelik visited Jerusalem he brought with him to Abyssinia a number of Priests, and according to the story, they got a perfect model of the Ark made, which they put in the Temple, and carried off the original.[8-12]

No one is allowed to enter. One holy monk ventured in and was struck dead. Two young and pure boys were sent in and according to their account there are five veils, and the Ark is within the fifth. It rests upon a four footed erection of pure gold, like a large stool or a bed, and the Ark itself is of gold and precious stones, resplendent with light. The church is a Sanctuary. Any one committing murder, if he reaches it, is safe from his pursuers.[8-13]

The people of Adowah are all very pleased about the fate of Theodore. They have got a correct account of events, but afterwards all sorts of absurd rumours followed, one of which was that 6000 of our soldiers had been killed in battle. The truth had been now confirmed and credited, but they could not understand by what means Queen Victoria could be made certain of the truth, for we had not brought off the head of Teodorus, nor his hair or any other portion of his body to send to England as evidence. They were very much astonished to learn that the Queen Victoria already had received the news, and believed it, and had sent back her congratulations to Sir Robert Napier and his soldiers.[8-14]

In the evening I had a bath at the waterfall at this place. Under the fall there is a pool surrounded by rocks with bushes, flowers, and ferns, and into the clear cold water I took a header. I found I could swim without danger from the rocks at the bottom, for in the most of it I could feel no ground. I swam under the fall and had a shower bath.

At Goun-Gouna there is a church built on a ledge of the perpendicular rock high up above the village.[8-15] I climbed up to see it, and found the way most difficult, only fit for monkeys. The ledge of rock once reached the way was easy. The church is very small, and under its porch there is a basin dug in the rock which is supplied by some spring of water. It is clear and cool and I put my head into it to get a good drink. There are ferns along the ledge and a ruined building or two. This church is said to have been founded by a St. Libanos whose shrine is in a rude building in the cliff.[8-16]

24 May, Sun. Senafe. We have again returned to what might almost be called the real starting point of the Expedition, and we have here returned to many creature comforts which are acceptable to all. Senafe is crowded with tents, and troops. We wait here a few days in order to let the regiments proceed down for embarcation, and to enable Sir Robert Napier to meet Kasa who is reported to be on the way not far off from this.

On the 20th another flood came down upon the Sooroo pass and partially destroyed the road, and drowned 5 mule drivers, and a number of the mules.

PART IX: SENAFE TO ZOULLA - 25 MAY TO 2 JUNE

25 May, Mon. Senafe. Review and Races to-day. Kasa arrived in the afternoon.

26 May, Tues. Senafe. Sir Robert Napier received Kasa to-day, and is to leave with him a lot of old smooth bore muskets, ammunition etc.[9-1] This is done in the hope that it may strengthen Kasa's power, and by enabling him to dominate, to give peace and stability to Abyssinia, and avoid that anarchy which all naturally fear will [be] the consequence of our leaving the country. Kasa expressed fears of Egypt, but no promise could be given on our part regarding that power.[9-2] All will leave this by the 29th, and the Q.M.G. [Quarter Master General] Dept. expect that by the 10th of June all will have quitted Zoulla.

DAJAZMACH KASA, RULER OF TEGRAY

Simpson elaborates on his talks with Dajazmach Kasa:

At Senafe, Kasa, Prince of Tegray, came to meet Sir Robert, and we waited there for a day or so while a review took place, at which Kasa was present. This was on May 24th, the Queen's birthday. Sir Robert gave a dinner in the evening. Kasa did not attend that. One day I went to Kasa's camp and took his portrait. This, although only in pencil, Sir Robert declared was the best likeness he had ever seen. Probably this was owing to the peculiar and marked features of the man, which were easily caught. In Kasa's tent I was treated to *tej,* [9-3] a kind of mead which the Abyssinians make. Kasa afterwards became

127

Negoosa Negyst, or King of the kings of Ethiopia, and assumed the name of John, or Johanna.

We left Prince Kasa at Senafe, but he sent some of his people with us down to Zoulla to receive some old rifles. (*Autobiography,* 195–196)

KASA ON THE THRONE

Having given almost every phase of Abyssinian life—having given the labourer in the field ploughing, and the domestic life of those who toil at the work of the cottage— it is fitting to complete the picture of life in Abyssinia to give the King upon his Throne.

When at Senafe the Commander-in-Chief asked Dajazmach Kasa to give me a sitting for his portrait, which was granted, I went over to the Abyssinian camp, and prominent among the rude tents of the soldiers I saw a large red one which I knew must have been that of Kasa.

On entering I found no furniture except a bedstead with two large cushions upon it, between which Kasa was sitting closely wrapped up in a *shama*, the white cotton shawl, with red stripe, which is worn by all the better classes of people. A carpet was placed on each side, in front of the bedstead and on this the principal chiefs sat, while behind stood the attendants. One had a *Chowrie*[9-4] to wave away flies and another held a bottle of tej, of which Kasa at times took a small taste. On the left hand of Kasa on the bedstead was placed a sword, and I recognised it as the one he had received in *durbar* [audience] from Sir Robert Napier. Underneath the bedstead, there was barely visible a gun and a belt of cartridges such as one sees worn by many Abyssinians.

After I had taken Kasa's portrait, and while he was looking at it, I made a general sketch of him on his throne and the figures around.

Although the face of Kasa is delicate and not indicative of much power, I noticed that this was not the case with his chiefs. Most of them were men with their heads grey and white, not plaited, but curly, giving some of them the appearance of the apostles in the cartoons of Raphael, the *shama*, or robe, being worn exactly as the figures given in the most of the old masters. These

128

KASA, PRINCE OF TEGRAY, SEATED IN STATE

men had all good features, with strong powerful bodies. At the end I was offered some tej to drink, and by means of the word *Salaam* I was able to let Kasa understand that I was drinking "towards his health."

The name of the throne and bedstead is the same word, which is *Alga*. They have another word *Zefan*.⁹⁻⁵

As an Abyssinian king seldom lives in a fixed abode this sketch in a tent may be taken as the normal condition of royal life in Abyssinia. Theodore is said never to have been happy except when in his tent, and amongst his soldiers moving about.

The well at the church of Goun-Gouna was beautifully fringed with ferns.

27 May, Wed. Senafe. This afternoon the Naval Rocket Brigade under Captain Fellowes went out and practised against the rocks at this place. Kasa and Sir Robert Napier came over to see the performance.

> ...Kasa was invited to come and see the performance of the Naval Rocket Brigade. This body was organised under Captain Fellowes, of H.M.S. *Dryad*. Its armament consists of twelve rocket-tubes; each tube can be carried upon a mule, with two boxes of ammunition. Within fifty or sixty seconds after the order is given to prepare for action, the tubes can be made all ready and the firing may begin.

> As these tubes can be so easily carried, their use in mountain warfare is evident; and in the present campaign they have done very good service. At Arogee these noisy missiles produced great consternation among Theodore's rash followers, and in the attack upon Magdala, on April 13, they were equally effective.

> The Brigade earned great praise from the Commander-in-chief; and their fame had spread throughout Abyssinia, so that Kasa was most anxious to see these terrible instruments of destruction. The brigade turned out, and a point was selected high up on the bare rock, which is so remarkable a feature in the Senafe landscape. This was made the point of attack; and it was wonderful to see how near to that point every rocket went.

The Naval Rocket Brigade Firing Rockets at Seneffe

131

Sir Robert Napier led Kasa by the hand, and had the rockets and their action explained to him. The principal chiefs of the Tegray were there, and all manifested the greatest astonishment at what they saw. General Florente and Count Mirasol, the Spanish officers who lately reached the camp, were also on the ground, and expressed their admiration at the performance of the Naval Brigade. (*ILN*, published 11 July 1868.)

It is rumoured that the Commander-in-Chief is to return to England and that Dajazmach Alamayou is to go with him instead of going to Bombay.

28 May, Thurs. Senafe. In the afternoon Kasa's people came over and went through a number of performances peculiar to Abyssinia, such as riding and throwing sticks at one another.

29 May, Fri. Rayry Guddy. At 10 o'clock we marched from Senafe. Kasa came and accompanied Sir Robert to the top of the Ghat which is the boundary of Abyssinia. At this point some slight ceremony was gone through: a man of the 4th exhibited the action of the Snider and Colonel Dillon* fired off an American repeater with about 8 shots. A salute was fired with two of the mule mountain guns and Sir Robert bid Kasa goodbye wishing "that God would prosper him and enable him to do good to his country" and in a few minutes or so afterwards he and all his force were out of Abyssinian territory.

30 May, Sat. Undel Wells. Came in this morning with Major Roome* and the advanced guard, inspecting the road for Shohos. This was done on account of the murdering of Mr. Dufton,* and one of his servants, and the looting of Sir Charles Staveley's butler, of which we got more particulars at this place.[9-6] I found my old friends of the 25th Bombay Native Infantry here, and found Dufton's grave close to their mess tent, where Stewart, Fellowes and I slept coming up the pass.

31 May, Sun. Sooroo. The 25 Native Infantry, with Major Roome and Mr. Munzinger,*[9-7] went up the hills to look for Dufton's murderers. One Shoho that had been apprehended threw a stone at a Sepoy and then tried to run away, but he was instantly shot.[9-8] Then spent the whole day in searching but found no one. We heard many details of the murder. A spear had been thrown at Dufton which penetrated through his body. They then mutilated him by sword cuts. He lived all through the night and died at 9.15 the next morning. We also got details of the flood on the 19th at Sooroo. It came down at about 15 minutes notice. Arbuthnot made a narrow escape; he was going down the pass at the time.

1 June, Mon. Koomaylee. Found the road very much altered, very bad, scarce a road visible. Various reports of an attack by Shohos at lower Sooroo. Found Koomaylee very dusty.

2 June, Tues. Zoulla. The Commander-in-Chief and Head Quarter Staff came by special train this morning. We had one of the carriages filled with Abyssinians, who sat discussing with themselves, as to whether Solomon could possibly have known of such a means of travelling.

Simpson later recalled that, on reaching Koomaylee, he and his friends found that:

On our return a rude kind of railway had been laid down. The stock for it was a contractor's material that had been brought from India. The only carriages were the waggons the contractors had used for railway making. On our arrival at the Koomaylee terminus a "special train" was arranged for Sir Robert and the Headquarters party. Planks had been laid across the waggons, and, if I recollect right, a flag—a Jack, or something of that kind—was laid on the planks Sir Robert occupied. Speedy was in the same waggon with me, and a few of Kasa's men were in the next "carriage." They did not have seats, but squatted down on the floor. Some of these people had to walk, and when we passed them they tried by hard running to keep up with us, but were soon left behind, much to the amusement of their friends in the waggon. I noticed that they were conversing among themselves very earnestly, and I asked Speedy to inquire what their thoughts were. They said they were considering "whether Solomon in all his glory had ever conceived such a wonderful method of travelling as this." They had no doubt been thinking of Solomon's wonderful throne, on which the genii carried him through the air. (*Autobiography*, 196)

In his "Artist's Jottings," Simpson continues:

About the state of education among the Abyssinians I had little means of forming an opinion. Many can read and write. They are all well acquainted with the characters and events of the Old and New Testament history, and they often refer to them for illustration.

We had a very characteristic example of this on our return; we were coming by the railway which had been constructed between Zoulla and Koomaylee; some of the head men of Tegray had come down to the latter place, and the Commander-in-Chief invited them to Zoulla to see what would be to them the wonders of that place. They were placed in a carriage with their followers, under charge of Captain Speedy, who could act as interpreter. Like most Orientals, the Abyssinians endeavour to conceal their feelings of astonishment, but a railway was too much for them. The first thing to produce excitement was one of their own people they saw making for Zoulla on the dusty road; he made a vain effort to keep up with the train, and the shouts of laughter which followed was more like a return from the Derby than the conduct of placid Easterns.

This was followed by a great deal of loud and animated conversation, and on inquiries being made as to its import, we learned that they were discussing the question as to "whether Solomon in all his glory ever could have conceived such a mode of travelling as this railway." So far as we could make out, it seemed that this "Board of Inquiry" were coming to conclusions rather adverse to Solomon's knowledge on the subject. "See," said a warm and very practical admirer of the railway system, "one could go to sleep and travel at the same time." This gentleman's knowledge of the matter, and his notions of sleeping accommodation, may be guessed, when it is stated that he had little more than standing-room when he spoke, but in that space he had managed to double up his knees to his chin, and there is no doubt but he could in this sitting posture have managed to sleep, and comfortably too, for him.

At the end of this discussion Captain Speedy suggested to them that possibly "the Ingleese were the true descendants of Menelik and the Queen of Sheba, to whom all the wisdom of Solomon had come down." And on that day, when these chiefs had drunk the condensed water of the sea, and seen the vast vessels like cities full of people afloat, the great engines which moved them, the heavy guns of the men-of-war, which were fired especially for their edification, when they had walked all over some of the large transport steamers and seen the cabin accommodation, which went far beyond their notions of things terrestrial, they might well have been willing to admit, that if the wisdom of Solomon applied to material things, we could at least show good signs of having had a fair share of the inheritance. (*Jottings*, 613)

Heat and dust is very troublesome.

3 June, Wed. Zoulla. Hard at work writing for the post. Baths in the sea at the Bundar [waterfront] every evening.

4 June, Thur. Zoulla.

5 June, Fri. Zoulla.

6 June, Sat. Went in the morning with Lockhart* to see the ancient Adulis.

7 June, Sun. Zoulla. Got a note from my old friend Froin of the *Star of the South*, Balaclava, and went on board of the present ship, the *Queen of the South*, bathed and dined.**9-9**

8 June, Mon. Zoulla. Breakfasted on board the *Koina*, Tiffin on board the *Feroze*. Dinner on the *Queen of the South*. Great Dinner on board the Turkish Frigate.

9 June, Tue. Zoulla. Early this morning I started and got on board the *Feroze* with my "kit."

10 June, Wed. On board the *Feroze* all day. About 8 a.m. Sir Robert, with Dillon, Thesiger* and Scott* came on board. In the afternoon I went with Sir Robert on board the *Octavia* to see the commodore. In the Evening a dinner on board the *Feroze*. Com. Heath, Captain Tryon,* General Russell*, Gen. Merewether, Lockhart, etc. were of the invité.

PART X: ANNESLEY BAY TO LONDON
11 June to 2 July, 1868

11 June, Thur. At 7 a.m. we started and were soon out of sight of Zoulla. Very hot and hazy. At 10 p.m. we came to an anchor.

12 June, Friday. By 4 a.m. we were again under weigh, and got out of the mass of islands. Saw land in the west for the most of the day, but in the afternoon it was lost in the haze.

13 June, Sat. The wind blew very strong all night, much cooler, and this morning the change was still more marked.

14 June, Sun. The party on Board the *Feroze* were:

> Capt. Arnot, captain of the *Feroze*
> Sir Robert Napier
> Capt. Scott, A.D.C.
> Capt. Holland,* Q. M. Gen. Dept.
> Capt. Speedy
> Dajazmach Alamayou, son of Theodore
> Count Seckendorff, Prussian Army
> Capt. Kodolitsch, Austrian Army, and servant Joseph
> Lord Charles Hamilton, A.D.C. and servant Chandria
> Mr. Holmes of the British Museum.
> Dr. Austin, *Times* correspondent [10-1]
> Col. Dillon, Military Secretary.
> Wm. Simpson, *Illustrated London News* correspondent
> Capt. Tweedy, Political Department
>   (and contributor to *Blackwood's Magazine*)
> Col. Thesiger, Adjutant General of the Expedition
> Major Roberts
> Captain Holland
> Captain Arbuthnot[10-2]

Simpson, in his Autobiography, *has much more to say about Alamayou, and his history on board ship:*

It had at first been arranged to send Theodore's Queen and her son to India, but upon her death it was determined to bring Alamayou to England. The boy was placed in charge of Captain Speedy, and at Zoulla the two joined our mess. This was a great change for the little fellow, as a European table and all its details were new to him. His fingers had been his knife and fork previously. He chanced to sit beside me on the first morning at breakfast, and I remember how I gave him his first lesson in manipulating bread and marmalade. He had not the faintest notion what to do with these articles when placed upon his plate.

At last he was sent on board the *Feroze,* an Indian steamer that was to take Sir Robert Napier and the Headquarters party to Suez. (*Autobiography,* 198)

....A few Abyssinian servants were brought to attend upon him. Among others was a priest named Alika Zenub,[10-3] who was to be his tutor. One night on the Red Sea, before we reached Suez—we all slept on deck on account of the heat—a considerable noise was heard among Alamayou's party. Speedy went to them, and brought the boy away. It would seem they had tried to frighten him, for what purpose I did not quite comprehend.[10-4]

He slept beside Speedy that night, and next morning would not look at one of his people. Speedy asked him what was to be done with his servants. He gave a significant jerk with his hand to the gunwale of the vessel, and said, "Throw them into the sea." When these words were reported every one made the comment, "A chip of the old block." I believe the servants, including Alika Zenub, were all sent back to their own country from Suez. (*Autobiography,* 200)

15 June, Mon. Met the *Salsotte* about noon, stopped and we got letters, and papers.[10-5]

16 June, Tues. Saw land on the African side at various points, passed two islands called the Brothers.

17 June, Wed. The Captain or Pilot made a mistake about the entrance to the Gulph of Suez. It was difficult to make out which was the island of Shadwan. Time was lost.

18 June, Thurs. Got to an anchor about 10.39 a.m. Went on shore about 2 p.m.

> I went on shore with Speedy and Alamayou at Suez. We soon had a crowd at our heels when it was known that we had the son of Theodore with us. Speedy's object was to buy some clothes for himself and for Alamayou, so we entered a shop; but the difficulty, in a place like Suez, was to find garments for two such extreme customers. Speedy was 6 feet 6 inches, and the boy was only seven years. Speedy did find a pair of trousers that he could wear, but they suggested to my eye that he had grown a little out of them. Alamayou was more easily rigged out, and in that shop I saw him for the first time in elastic-side boots. A curious thing for a young savage. (*Autobiography*, 200–201)

19 June, Fri. Left Suez by a Special train with Sir Robert Napier and Staff, about 10.30 p.m.

20 June, Sat. Got to Cairo about 3. 30 a.m. and into Alexandria at 9 a.m.

21 June, Sun. Went in a search for the Coptic church. Found a Jewish Synagogue, near to Cleopatra's needle, and the Coptic church was close by. I could not discover much resemblance to the Abyssinian churches, visited the Roman and Greek churches, went on board the Troop Ship *Urgent* at 1/2 past 5 p.m.

22 June, Mon. Sir Robert Napier came on board early, between 6 and seven a.m. and we were under way for Malta.

> From Alexandria the *Urgent*, a Government troopship, took us to Malta. On board this ship Sir Robert had a ball made, and tried to get Alamayou

to play with him. If Sir Robert threw the ball, the youngster scarcely tried to catch it, and Sir Robert had to go and pick it up himself. Speedy asked him why he did not run for the ball. His answer was, "Am I not a king's son, why should I go and fetch it?" (*Autobiography,* 201)

23 June, Tue. Passed a screw steamer on our portside.

24 June, Wed.

25 June, Thur. Arrived at Malta about 7 p.m.

26 June, Fri.

Simpson continues his observations of Alamayou:

At Malta we had evidence that he was very sharp. Lord Clarence Paget* was then Commander-in-Chief in the Mediterranean, and Speedy was asked to take Alamayou to Lord Clarence's house, as his wife and children would like to see him. As Lord Clarence was an old Black Sea friend, I went with Speedy.

The children brought in all their toys, and even offered them to Alamayou, but he sat calm and sedate, not unlike the figures of Buddha. He appeared to take no notice of anything. Among the toys was one of a cat that played on a harp. The children thought it would interest, but he only gazed at it with an expression of supreme indifference. Kasa, Speedy's servant,[10-6] an Abyssinian, was in the next room waiting, so I took the cat and harp to show it to him. He became wild with excitement, and said to Speedy in Abyssinian, "How in the name of the Father, Son, and Holy Ghost, can you people teach cats to do such things?" The contrast between Kasa and Alamayou was most striking.

Here comes the sharpness of the boy. When we left, Speedy asked him if he was not surprised at the cat, and he said No, he saw it went with a screw, because he had given a slight wave of the hand, and the cat did not wink, so he knew it was not real. These illustrations of his conduct, which came under my eyes, may indicate his character and capabilities. (*Autobiography*, 201)

27 June, Sat. Sailed about 8.30 a.m.

28 June, Sun. African coast in sight, Bay of Tunis, and by night, the southern part of Sardinia was on our Starboard.

29 June, Mon. No land to-day, saw a whale. A storm ahead of us at Sunset.

30 June, Tue. Got in during the night to Marseille, landed at 10 a.m. and left by the train at 11.30. Dined at Lyons.

1 July, Wed. Got into Paris at 7 a.m. and left again in the evening at 7.30 [p.m.]. Was introduced to our Ambassador, Lord Lyons,[10-7] on the platform of the railway station.

2 July, Thur. Dover at 4 a.m. An address and grand reception to Sir Robert Napier. Bid him good bye at Herne Hill station, and back to 64 Lincon's Inn Fields about 7 a.m.

> The Queen, I understood, took charge of the boy, and confirmed Speedy as his Comptroller. They lived for some years at Freshwater, Isle of Wight. Speedy got an appointment in India, somewhere in Oudhe, and took Alamayou there. On his return the Queen presented a gold watch to Speedy as a mark of her appreciation of his services, and the boy was placed under a tutor. He died at Leeds of consumption, and was buried, I think, in St. George's Chapel, Windsor, in October, 1879.[10-8] His age at his death would be seventeen or eighteen at the most. (*Autobiography,* 201–202)

APPEⲚDⲒXES

APPENDIX A:

THE DESIGN OF THE ABYSSINIAN MEDAL

Editor's Note: Simpson started his diary with an account of his part in designing a medal for soldiers in the campaign (see back cover). We have separated it from the main narrative, and included additional material from his Autobiography.

The origin of the design was from some officers one day in Lockhart's tent, which I shared on the return march,—expressing an enquiry, "Shall we get a medal for this campaign?" I said that the best thing to do was to design the medal, and getting a scrap of paper, I knocked it off. It required only a day or so for the news to spread that we were to get a medal—the "shame" [rumour] being based on this sketch. During the morning's march I was repeatedly accosted by officers coming to me and asking to see the design of the medal "that we are all to receive." Lord Napier at last heard "that we were all to get medals," and sent for me to bring the design. He was pleased with it, and asked me to make some alterations, and he sent it home from Abyssinia.

> *Simpson, who took considerable pride in his design for the medal, subsequently referred to its conception and explains more fully how his original design had been modified.*

I knew that every one was against the "half-crown" design which had been rigidly adhered to in all war medals. So I made a sketch. Almost every detail of the design was derived from Abyssinian sources. The general design was an Abyssinian cross—of bronze, I suggested—with the Queen's head of silver in the centre. The ribbon had a red stripe horizontally. This was taken from the shama, a large sheet with a red stripe near one of its edges, a dress of honour—in fact, a sort of court dress in Abyssinia. Every one in the Expedition was familiar with it, and recognised its appropriateness. To the clasp, with the word "Magdala" on it, I added small pendants, characteristic of Abyssinian jewellery.

It soon was known that a design had been made. It was even rumoured that it was settled all were to receive medals. Our tent became thronged with those that wanted to see the design. Even men I did not know came up to me on the march and asked as a favour to see it. Sir Robert heard of it, and I had to take it to him. He was delighted with it, and suggested some small alterations. These I made, and then did a very careful drawing, which he took home, and submitted to the Government when the question of a medal came up for consideration. I believe he tried hard to make them adopt a design like mine. He sent for me in London, and I twice over made alterations in the detail, which he hoped would make it acceptable. But he failed. This was explained to me by the suggestion that the high officials who have the settling of these matters all wear orders or crosses on their breasts, and any mere war medal beyond the traditional half-crown pattern they think might be mistaken for one of those higher orders of decoration. Hence their rigid adherence to the old type.

I learned afterwards that the Princess Louise made the design which was actually adopted. She was limited to the half-crown shape, but there are still traces of my design in the medal. The Queen's head is within a contracted circle, and what formed the cross in my sketch became a zig-zag line or scallop, with the letters of the word "Abyssinia" between the points. In one of the designs I introduced a crown above the medal. As there is some difficulty in producing ribbons with cross stripes, the red band was put perpendicularly instead of horizontally as I had it. (*Autobiography*, 196–98)

I may mention that I am indebted to Lord Napier and Colonel Dillon for receiving the Abyssinia Medal. When I met them at Delhi, in 1876, they were surprised to hear I had not got one, and they at once took steps, which led to it being given to me—Wm. Simpson.

APPENDIX B:

Simpson's visits to churches

*Sections from the diary and Simpson's later writings concerning
the beliefs, religious services, and architecture of Ethiopian
churches are grouped here for easier reference.*

Plan of the Church of St. Miriam at Focada [Visited 2 April]

I send you the plan of this church as I think it gives—with others sent—
about all the varieties in plan that I have visited [in] in this country.

It will be seen that although a square church, it differs materially from the
one at Adigerat. The main points of distinction being that the three courts
are placed the one behind the other, and the *Makdas* from this arrangement,
is not surrounded by the *Kudist* or second court, but is a distinct building to
the east. Another peculiarity is the existence of a space to the east of the
Tabot, and a room upon each side of it.[B-1] All the information I could get
respecting them was that they were used by the priests for putting on their
vestments.

This part of the construction suggests that there must be some link of
connection between this plan and that of the rock-cut church at Dongolo. I
would suggest that it presents the link between the Greek form of church
brought over by the first missionaries, and the Jewish type which was added,
and which seems at last to have prevailed as the favourite plan with the
Abyssinians.

In some churches there is a door to the east of the Tabot. None are without
a window, and it receives either the name "The Gate of Light," or "The
Window of Light" as the case may be.

When it is a door, it is always closed or built up—and only the small window
is left. This is no doubt done in accordance with Ezekiel, which states that

when the Angel brought him to this gate which is towards the east, that it was shut. "Then said the Lord unto me. This gate shall be shut, it shall not be opened, and no man shall enter it by it; because the Lord, the God of Israel hath entered by it. Therefore shall it be shut." Ez. 44:9.

At the church I got the names for East, West, South and North; they are *Miserack, Merab, Deboub, and Samian.* B-2

Church at Adigerat [Visited on Palm Sunday, 5 April]

I managed to reach the church very shortly after the day had dawned, and I found a number of men in the outer court, on the Beatalehem side, singing psalms; each man held a long stick in his hand, with a cross piece on the top; they are longer, but exactly like the staffs used in the Greek Church; but instead of being ornamental, like those, they are simple sticks cut from the tree. Some had drums exactly like the Indian tom-tom, and they all swung their bodies and raised them up and down to the tune, striking the end of the sticks into the ground, and at times clapping their hands. The music seemed rather wild and harsh; from this and the action of all their bodies moving there was a feeling as if they were in anger and were deprecating something or other.

There were not many people present. I found a few, sitting and standing. On the women's side of the second court I could not see much about then, for it was rather dark in that part of the church.

By-and-by the priests began to put on their robes, and this they did in the Holy of Holies. These are very simple, and I think they were put on over their robes, but the younger ones had merely a coarse red mantle.

The first part of the ceremony was to present bits of the palm to every one present; some had long full branches, others had only a few leaves. I was the only stranger present, and they presented me with a small piece, which I stuck in my button-hole. The *Alaki* [Alika] or chief priest of the church did not take part in these or any of the proceedings which followed; he only seemed, as far as I could see, to lead the psalm-singing in the outer place.

The priests now all came out of the Holy of Holies by the Beatalehem side door, and, going round to the front door on the outside of the church, began that part of the ceremony represented in my sketch. A very large copy of the Scriptures in Coptic [in fact, Ge'ez], written on sheepskin, and well bound in brown leather, was held up by two of the younger clergy. One of the older priests stood before it with a richly-ornamented wooden cross, which he held in his right hand, as if presenting it to the book; in his other hand he held, like the others, a branch of palm. He read a portion of the book. I noticed that at times he was not quite sure of the words; and more than once I heard him prompted and corrected in his reading by those around him. This does not indicate a great deal of scholarship among the priests of this Church.

After the reading, what I took for a psalm was sung. Beside this priest there stood a robed attendant with incense, in a very richly-ornamented censer. Another stood with a large cross, made of brass, on the end of a pole; the cross had the crescent underneath it, this being a common arrangement in the Eastern Church. A boy carried a bell, which was well used through the ceremony.

After this was finished, they all marched in an irregular procession—priests and people all mixed together—round to the door on the women's side of the church. This door was kept shut during the whole of the morning. Here a similar ceremony was gone through. Then they went as before to the eastern end. Here there was no door; a double door had been constructed, but had been built up into two small windows. Here, again, the same performance was enacted. They came round to the Beatalehem door, which was open all the time, and again they went through the same ceremony. This circumambulation of the church must have occupied about three quarters of an hour.

Shortly afterwards the bread and wine was brought from the Beatalehem. The bread was in a basket covered with a red cloth, and carried on the head of one of the younger attendants. The wine was in a flagon, which was also covered with a red cloth. I call it wine, although it really was not so, being only the juice of raisins, called by them *Dam*, or "blood."

Instead of entering the Holy of Holies by the Beatalehem side, they only entered the outer door; there and then they passed round in the second court and entered the sanctuary by the front door. The front door had been shut all the time, but the door of the Beatalehem side was occasionally open, so that I could see a little. The ark was covered all over with cloth, which, I suppose, would be removed when the consecration of the elements took place. None of this ceremony was visible, for they carefully shut the doors. It was a very prolonged rite, and must have occupied an hour. We could hear the music, and reading, and chanting. But most of it seemed to be sound only, without even an attempt at articulating words, and the music seemed more like the wailing of pain than sounds of joy and gladness.

At one part of the ceremony some of them came out of the sanctuary and went round with the incense, and incensed the people; another held one of the wooden crosses, about a foot long, which he presented to each to kiss. He also presented it to me, and, like the others, I complied with the ceremony; so that, in the language of the day, I may now say that I have manifested a strong leaning to the forms of the Coptic [in fact, Ethiopian Orthodox] Church. A small taper, for a candle, was carried along with the cross. At times the people were very silent, and bowed towards the sanctuary. As a rule, during the service they behaved in a very quiet manner—not exactly in the way the congregation of a Western church behave. They went about; some repeated prayers and used the rosary, while others sat in groups chatting. The women never moved out of their place, but sat on the floor. A few of the men took to psalm-singing, led by the Alika. (*ILN,* 9 May 1868)

General Notes on the Ethiopian Church and its possible relationship with Judaism

Simpson was fascinated by the Judaic influences on the Ethiopian church and the prevalence of Hebrew words in Ethiopia, and also by the legend of the Queen of Sheba. This extended selection is from his "Jottings."

It is not an easy task to account for the Jewish traditions that prevail in Abyssinia, or offer a clear and credible explanation of their origin and meaning. For instance, there is the origin of the race through Solomon and the Queen of Sheba;[B-3] or the still stranger legend of the real ark being carried off from Jerusalem to Aksum. Besides, there are large Jewish colonies in Abyssinia, and a great number of Hebrew words and names are to be found in the language of the country. These words are not derived from the Hebrew, as is the case in other languages, but are the actual words themselves. According to the now received classification, the ancient Ethiopian is, like the Hebrew, a Semitic language. This might account for some identity between the two, but, strange to say, the Jews, or Falashas, as they are called, do not speak Hebrew.[B-4] Their language is as wide of the Hebrew as the Amharic or the other dialects of Abyssinia. It is evident that this fact must complicate the whole question, not only of language, but of race.

It would perhaps be unfair to be critical upon such a story as that of the Queen of Sheba and her son Menelik, but it clearly fails in its purpose of explaining the origin of the Abyssinians. A queen implies a country and a people, and thus we have the race existing before its origin and the birth of its founder. The story of Menelik, indeed, is told in another way, which brings it more within the limits of credibility. According to this version, he was sent to Jerusalem for his education, and upon returning to Abyssinia, Solomon prevailed on the Jews of Palestine to send each his first-born son along with him, and this is the source to which everything Jewish is generally attributed.[B-5]

The story of the ark is worth giving, for it is not so well known. When Menelik was leaving Jerusalem he induced a number of the chief priests to accompany him,[B-6] and they, being strongly averse to leaving behind them all the glory and divine protection which they believed to accompany the presence of the ark, conceived the idea of making an imitation of it. This, from their position in the temple, they were able to do, and they carried off the real ark, leaving the other in its place. It is the belief of the Abyssinians that it remains in the church of Aksum to this day. No one is allowed to see it but the Abuna, or head of the Abyssinian Church, who is the equivalent of the high priest. The Governor of Aksum is still called *Naberada,* or "Keeper of the Ark."[B-7]

They have also a curious legend about the celebrated obelisk at Aksum. The sons of Noah, when they separated to the three ancient divisions of the world, erected obelisks as memorials of the event. Japhet did so in Europe, Shem in Asia, and Ham, or Cham, in Africa, this last being the one still standing at Aksum.[B-8]

The lion on Theodore's seal, that with which he sealed his letters to the British Government, is the lion of Judah. The words of the motto, in Amharic, are *Moa anbasa saoemoeagada Juda,* which is translated, "The lion of the race of Judah has triumphed." A similar seal with the lion upon it has been assumed by Kasa, Prince of Tegray, since Theodore's death.[B-9]

But the strongest feature of all is, the curious mixture of Judaism with the Christianity of Abyssinia. This is perhaps most evident in the construction of their churches. They are formed upon the threefold division of the Tabernacle and the Temple....The inner sanctuary is called the *makdas,* the second is the *kudist,* and the outer is the *kunyéh-mahelet.* The two first of these words are clearly Hebrew, *mikdash* being a term sometimes applied to the whole of the temple, and sometimes only to the holy place. From kodish came *kudish-kudishim,* the usual name of the sanctuary in Hebrew, and identical with the kudist of the Abyssinian Church.

In the makdas, or holy of holies, there is what is called the ark, or tabot. This is formed of four wooden posts, placed about two feet asunder, and about seven or eight feet in height. Near the middle there is a shelf tied to the posts, and other pieces laid across. The whole of the wood is untrimmed by axe or knife. This is called the *menber,* or table, upon which the elements are laid for consecration. It is covered with a cloth, and under the cloth is placed a square pieces of alabaster, or marble, rudely ornamented with crosses. This they explain as being the representative of the stones of the Law, and typical of the "new stone." Between the altar and the front door is suspended a curtain, which in many cases was nothing more than a piece of matting or dirty cloth; this is the veil, and it prevents those on the outside from seeing the ark when the front door is open.

There are usually four doors to the sanctuary, but the eastern door is always built up, with the exception of a small window. It is called "the door of light." The explanation of this may be found in Ezek. 44:1, 2. The door of the outer court is also built up in the same way as the inner. All the Abyssinian churches are constructed with the altar towards the east.

There is always at the north-east corner of the church a small building, generally only a few yards from the church; this is the Beatalehem or "House of Bread." It is here that the priests prepare the bread for the sacrament; hence its name. It is a curious coincidence that the Hebrew word Bethlehem should signify "House of Bread," and that the Arabs should render it Beit-lahm, or "House of Flesh." The Abyssinian Church teaches the doctrine of the real presence, although Bruce mentions one priest who expressed doubts to him upon the subject. The bread used in the church is a cake baked on an earthen griddle, and is called by the Hebrew and Arabic word *korban*, or "sacrifice." The wine is not fermented, being only raisins steeped in water. This they call *dam*, the Hebrew word for "blood;" it is also prepared in the Beatalehem.

The Abyssinian Church being so thoroughly Eastern, the separation of sexes might be expected to be one of its features. This practice is supposed by many to have some very deep signification and spiritual meaning; but any one acquainted with Eastern customs can easily give the explanation. There is nothing spiritual about it; it is only a form which dates back to the time when there was no social intercourse between the sexes. Women were separated in the house as well as in the church. A harem necessitates a separate place of prayer. All Mohammedan mosques are so arranged; Solomon's temple had its women's court; and a Jewish synagogue ought to be so constructed that the women and men should not see each other. In Abyssinia there is no separation of the sexes in the usual intercourse of life, and, so far as I saw, it seemed to be only nominally retained in church. The south side of the church is called the women's side, and the door is called the women's door. The northern side is for the men, but it is not so named. It is the "Beatalehem side" and the door is the Beatalehem door, because the bread and wine come in from that side to the sanctuary.

In most cases there is a burial-place around the church, and the whole is enclosed with a wall. The door of this wall is called the *deja-salaam*, which is "the gate of peace," or "the gate of bowing down," for Abyssinians in entering or passing a church will bow down at the outer gate, and kiss the wall.

As a rule, these churches are mere sheds, constructed of wood and wattles, and a conical thatched roof. The wall of the holy of holies is always plastered with mud. The floor is littered with straw, and is usually in a very untidy state. Roughly-made coffins are to be found in many churches with the bones of holy men, and in some the bones are wrapped up in skins.

Here and there a finer church is to be found, and in some cases decorated with pictures. Those of Chelicut and Adigerat are so distinguished. The art is rude and primitive. Indian officers always declared that these works had a striking resemblance to the pictures of native artists of India. The absence of shadow, a total disregard of perspective, and the making of a king three or four times the size of those around him, are all points which produce this impression of similarity. B-10

The Virgin and Child is a very favourite subject; the Crucifixion is represented much as it is in European pictures. St. George is a highly popular saint, and generally occupies a prominent place, riding on a very white horse with a green dragon under him. In the Adigerat church there was a very curious picture of Pharaoh. Pharaoh is on his horse in the Red Sea, and Moses stands on the bank, holding a great cross in his left hand, while the right is held up as if in the act of reproaching. The cross represented is exactly the same as those used in the Abyssinian churches at the present day, and it shows that the pre-Christian origin of that symbol seemed to be a settled point with the artist; and if his archeology is to be trusted, it will also be interesting information to Biblical students to learn that Pharaoh's hosts were armed with muskets.

The saints, and their various modes of martyrdom, are standard subjects in all church decoration. They remind one a good deal of a "chamber of horrors." We found that we could understand the names of the saints as pronounced by the priest. The Greek form of the words are still retained. Thus they say "Ioannes," "Petros," "Paowlus", "Bartolomeus," etc. The

Virgin they call "Miriam," and Jesus is "Yasous." Before each of these names, they use the word kudosh, evidently derived from the Hebrew for holy: thus they say "Kudosh Gabriel" or the Holy Gabriel, or "Kudosh Gergius" for St. George. Kudosh Kirkos is a very favourite saint, and many churches are dedicated to him. He is said to be a boy saint....

Church of St. Gabriel (Kydoos Gabriel) near Takazze [Visited 26 April]

I stopped into a church one morning near the Takazze, and hearing that the consecration service was going on, waited till the priests appeared at the door, bearing the consecrated elements. But no one came forward to partake: they stood for a few minutes on the steps singing as usual, and then returned into the sanctuary. Doubtless it was known that no one would be there to receive it that day. This could be inferred from the previous preparation required of the communicants, making it evident they considered the bringing forth of the bread and wine as an essential part of the ceremony. It is quite natural to think that they would look on it as typical of the sacrifice having been made and freely offered, and that its acceptance or rejection is a responsibility which belongs to those to whom the offer is presented.

While the priests are thus employed within, the laity are not idle without. So far as my short experience went, it seemed that very few people attended church. Of those a number are constantly engaged singing psalms. This is done in the outer court, whose name, Kunyéh-Mahlet, is derived from *mahlet*, a "song," "hymn," or "music." Each man holds a long stick, about six or seven feet in length, cut from the tree so as to have a cross on it at the top, like a pastoral staff; and in the other hand he has what I suppose, for want of a better name, must be called a musical instrument. It is a piece of bent iron with some other pieces strung upon it, so that they produce a jingling noise when moved up and down, and it is so very like the ancient Egyptian systrum that one can scarcely help coming to the conclusion that it is the lineal descendant of that instrument. The only other instrument that I saw was a drum, very like those used in India, and here, as there, beaten with the hands.[B-11] In singing, they form a circular group, standing with their faces towards the centre, and sway their bodies about, lifting their sticks high in the air and bringing the lower end down with considerable force upon the ground. I must say that they seemed to be intently earnest about it, although the strange performance seemed, rather laughable.

This service of the priests and that of the congregation go on together—the two forming a strange unconnected medley. Those who are not engaged in psalm-singing, stand about the church, or sit on the ground, or on some of the steps at the doors. Some repeat prayers; I saw one man standing at the Beatalehem door, who during the whole service continued muttering to himself with almost breathless speed, at the same time his fingers were busy with a rosary. The men moved about all over the church, with the exception of the sanctuary, but the women all sat quietly in the second court, on their own side. ("Jottings," 605–10)

APPENDIX C:

BRITISH MILITARY OFFICERS MENTIONED
(Using rank at time of Expedition)

Arbuthnot, Captain William – ADC to Expedition, Asst. Military Sec. to Sir Robert Napier; 43, 44, 47, 133, 136, 183

Armstrong, Major Charles – 10th Bengal Cavalry; 77

Baigrie, Major Robert (1829-1877) - Assistant Quarter Master General of Bombay Army and member of Reconnoitring Expedition under Sir Robert Napier; 1, 2

Bally, Captain William – ADC to General Collings; 33rd Duke of Wellington Regiment; 70

Beaumont, Captain William – Captain of a Transport Corps Division; 102nd Foot; 56

Beck, Lieutenant T. – commanding one Company of 21st Bombay Native Infantry (Marine Battalion); 53

Biddulph, General Sir Thomas Myddleton (1809–1878) – Keeper of the Queen's Privy Purse; 26, 34, 47, n iii-1 (165)

Campbell, Lieutenant Colonel Edward – Commander of 3rd Bombay Native Infantry; 82

Chamberlain, Major C. F. – Commanded 23rd Bengal Native Infantry; 48, 167

Chrystie, Captain William E. – In charge of engineering work at Zoulla and Sooroo Pass; 45, 56

Collings, Brigadier General John Elias, C.B. – Commanded a Brigade; Commanded Antalo Garrison; 70, 157, 158

Dillon, Colonel Martin A. – Military Secretary of Expedition; *later General, C.B;* 132, 135, 136, 144

Dufton, Henry – Civilian who had travelled extensively in Abyssinia; hired as interpreter by Intelligence Dept. of Expedition; 22, 25, 132–33, 162–64, 183

Fellowes, Captain Thomas Hounsom (1827–1923) – Commander of Naval

Rocket Brigade (Blue Jackets); *later, Rear Admiral;* 48, 53, 130, 132

Fraser, Colonel Charles Craufurd, VC (1829–1895) – 11th Hussars, Commandant at Napier HQ, in charge of all outposts along the route of march of the Expedition; 89

Goode, Lieutenant Elmhurst Roger. – Bombay Staff Corps; 54

Griffiths, Major Edward St. John – Infantry officer; 62

Hamilton, Cornet Lord Charles George Archibald – 11th Hussars; ADC to Lord Napier *(20 yrs. old at the time; Cornet was the lowest officer's rating in a cavalry regiment);* 88, 93,135

Heath, Captain Leopold George – Commander of Naval forces throughout the Expedition, based at Annesley Bay in his flagship, the frigate HMS *Octavia (later knighted, became Naval ADC to Queen Victoria);* 47, 110, 135

Hodges, Captain Thomas Trophimus – 76th Foot; Transport Officer and ADC to General Staveley; 80

Holland, Captain Trevenen J. – Assistant Quartermaster-General of Headquarters Staff; 114, 136, 162

Hore, Lieutenant Walter Stuart (1843–1918) – 25th Bombay Native Infantry; served on Commissariat Staff, in charge of Ashangi Depot; 77

Hozier, Lieutenant Henry M. – Assistant Military Secretary on Lord Napier's Headquarters Staff; 162

Little, Lieutenant Colonel Alfred Butler – Commander of 25th Bombay Native Infantry; 56

Lockhart, Lieutenant William Stephen Alexander – Bengal Staff Corps; 135, 143

Luckhardt, Lieutenant Wilhelm – Commissary staff of Bombay Army, assigned to Suez Depot; 44

Malcolm, Major General George – Commander of 2nd Division; 56, 70, 107

Merewether, Lieutenant Colonel William Lockyer (1825–1880) Political Officer of Expedition and Leader of Advance Force (known as the Reconnoitring Expedition); 113, 135

Milward, Lieutenant-Colonel Thomas Walter – Commander of one Artillery

Roberts, Captain Edward – 4th Foot (King's Own); 80, 113

Roome, Major Frederick (1829–1907)– Bombay Staff Corps; served on Intelligence Staff of Expedition; 132

Russell, Brigadier General Edward Lechmere – Commanding Officer, Zoulla Garrison; 12, 135

Scott, Lieutenant William Walter Hopton (1843–1916) (promoted to Captain during campaign) ADC to Lord Napier. Officer of Bengal Staff Corps; 135-36, 171

Speedy, Captain Charles – Personal staff of Lord Napier, Interpreter of Amharic; 23, 88, 133-34, 136-60, 164, 173, 184

Stansfeld, Major T. Wolrich – Officer of Madras Staff Corps; Commissariat Department, based at Suez; 43

Staveley, Major-General Sir Charles William Dunbar (1817–1896) – Commander of the First Division at Battle of Arogee and capture of Magdala; 88, 100, 132

Stewart, Brigadier General Donald Martin – Commander of the Second Division, Senafe Garrison; 47, 53, 132

Thacker, Major John – Commissariat Officer, serving under General Stewart at Senafe; 53

Thelwall, Major John B. – Commander of 21st Bengal Native Infantry; 53

Thesiger, Colonel Charles Wemyss (1831–1903) – Deputy Adjutant-General of Expedition, on Lord Napier's Headquarters staff. *(Son of Lord Chelmsford)*; 135, 136

de Thoren, Lieutenant Oscar William de Satge – Deputy Assist. Quarter Master General at Antalo, under General Collings; 70

Tryon, Captain George (1832–1893) – Naval Officer; Principal Transport Officer at Annesley Bay; *later Vice Admiral Sir George Tryon;* 135

Tweedie, Lieutenant William (1836–1914) – Bengal Staff Corps, Political Secretary on Lord Napier's Headquarters Staff; 136

Warburton, Lieutenant Robert (1843–1899) – probably Commissariat Dept. Officer *or* Transport Dept. Officer; 81

APPENDIX D:

SCHEDULE OF MARCHES FROM ZOULLA TO MAGDALA

[from Myatt, *March to Magdala*]

Stage	Distance	Cum. (miles)
Mileage		
Zoulla (Zulla, Zoolla)	—	—
Koomaylee (Kumayli)	14	14
Sooroo (Suru)	13	27
Undel Wells (Undul Wells)	13	40
Rayry Guddy (Rara Gudi)	17	57
Senafe (Senafé)	9	66
Goun-Gouna (Goon Goona)	12	78
Focada	14	92
Adigerat (Adigrat)	14	106
Mai Wahiz (Mai Wahez)	14	120
Ad Abaga (Adabaga)	17	137
Dongolo	10	147
Agoola (Agula)	10	157
Dolo	16	173
Eikhullet (Eikullet)	9	182
Antalo	12	194
Masgeh (Masgah)	9	203
Mashik	8	211
Attala (Atsala)	10	221
Bulago (Belago)	9	230
Makan	6	236
Ashangi	14	250
Mussagita (Mesagita)	8	258
Lat	7	265
Marawar (Marrawah)	10	275
Dildi (Dildee)	14	289
Wandach	8	297
Muja (Moja)	6	303
Takazze (Tacazze)	6	309
Santara	4	313
Gahso (Gaso)	11	324
Sindi	18	342
Bethor	7	349
Jedda Ravine (Djedda, Jidda)	6	355
Dalanta (Talanta)	9	364
Bashilo Ravine (Beshilo)	15	369
Magdala (Maqdala, Mäqdäla)	12	381

APPENDIX E:

BRiTiSH AND iNDiAN COMPANiES REPRESENTED ON THE EXPEDiTiON

CAVALRY: 3rd Dragoon Guards, 10th Regiment Bengal Lancers, 12th Regiment Bengal Lancers, 3rd Regiment Bombay Light Cavalry, 3rd Regiment Sind Horse.

ARTILLERY: G Battery, 14th Brigade Royal Artillery (Armstrong guns); A Battery 21st Brigade Royal Artillery, with mountain train; B Battery 21st Brigade Royal Artillery, with mountain train; 5th Battery 25th Brigade Royal Artillery, with mountain train; 1st Company Bombay Native Artillery; Naval Rocket Brigade: two batteries.

ENGINEERS: 10th Company Royal Engineers; Bombay Sappers and Miners: four companies; Madras Sappers and Miners: three companies.

INFANTRY: 4th Foot (King's Own Royal Regiment); 26th Foot (Cameronians); 33rd Foot (Duke of Wellington's); 45th Foot (Sherwood Foresters; 21st Bengal Native Infantry; 23rd Bengal Native Infantry (Punjabi Pioneers); 2nd Bombay Native Infantry (Grenadiers); 3rd Bombay Native Infantry; 5th Bombay Native Infantry; 8th Bombay Native Infantry; 10th Bombay Native Infantry; 18th Bombay Native Infantry; 21st Bombay Native Infantry; 25th Bombay Native Infantry; 27th Bombay Native Infantry (Baluchis).

∏otes:
BY SECTION AND PAGE NUMBERS

PREFACE: ARTISTIC ASPECTS (PAGES 1-4)

i-1.   As a sideline the photo team produced a series of views from the camp at Zoulla to Magdala, "illustrating points of interest on the line of march of the Army." (Trevenen J. Holland and Henry M. Hozier, *Record of the Expedition to Abyssinia* 2 (London, 1870), 345) They also made images of various personalities and groups involved from the campaign—ranging from Napier's staff to the captives they had come to rescue. Ultimately 78 of these pictures were made available to a limited public; presentation albums were assembled, and officers selected prints for their own personal enjoyment.

i-2.   Like all the correspondents with the Expedition, Simpson suffered not only from the lack of military action but from the length of time it took for his work to reach London. The further inland he went, the longer this lag time became; what was drawn on the Dalanta Plain on 21 and 22 April was not published in London until 6 June. This was true even though it probably was sent with the official army dispatches, which were carried by army horsemen at twice the speed which Simpson could have gone. The time from Dalanta to Annesley Bay was probably ten or eleven days by dispatch riders, then another 21 days from Annesley Bay to London; probably five weeks in all, or less from places closer to Annesley Bay.

INTRODUCTION: CAUSES AND CONSEQUENCES (PAGES 5-25)

ii-1.   For accounts of Ethiopia prior to the advent of Theodore, and his significance as an innovator, see Aristide Fanton, *L'Abyssinie lors de l'expédition anglaise, 1867–1868* (Paris, 1936); Donald Crummey, "Tewodros as Reformer and Modernizer," *Journal of African History,* 10 (1969): 3, 457–69; and Taddese Beyene, Richard Pankhurst and Shiferaw Bekele, *Kasa and Kasa: Papers on the Lives, Times and Images of Téwodros II and Yohannes IV, 1855–1889* (Addis Ababa, 1990), 3–144.

ii-2.   On Theodore's life see Sven Rubenson, *King of Kings: Tewodros of Ethiopia* (Addis Ababa, 1966), 2.

ii-3.   House of Commons, *Correspondence respecting Abyssinia 1848–1868* (London, 1868), 143–4 (hereafter cited as *Correspondence*).

ii-4.   Ibid, 150–1.

ii-5.   C. R. Markham, *A History of the Abyssinian Expedition* (London, 1869), 72.

ii-6.   Martino Mario Moreno, "La cronaca di re Teodoro attribuita al dabtarà 'Zaneb,'" *Rassegna di Studi Etiopici II* (1942): 1, 160–1.

ii-7.   Henry Dufton, *Narrative of a Journey Through Abyssinia in 1862–3* (London, 1867), 137.

ii-8.   On the work of the Chrischona missionaries see Donald Crummey, *Priests and Politicians: Protestant and Catholic Missions in Orthodox Ethiopia, 1830–1868* (Oxford, 1972), 115–28.

ii-9.   Tewodros' craftsmen had in fact made nine cannons, some of which (according to Markham, *History,* 367) had "neat inscription[s] in Amharic." On the casting of these cannons see Theophilus Waldmeier, *Erlebnisse in Abessinien* (Basel, 1896), 82–6 and 138–9. See also Dufton, *Narrative,* 84–5.

ii-10.   Henry Blanc, *A Narrative of Captivity in Abyssinia* (London, 1868), 342.

ii-11.   For detailed accounts of the negotiations between Theodore and the British government see Charles Tilstone Beke, *The British Captives in Abyssinia* (London, 1867); J. R. Hooker, "The Foreign Office and the Abyssinian Captives" *Journal of African History,* 2 (1961): 245–58; and Percy Arnold, *Prelude to Magdala: Emperor Theodore of Ethiopia and British Diplomacy* (London, 1992).

ii-12.   The original Amharic text, and an English translation of this letter, appear in Sven Rubenson, *Tewodros and his Contemporaries, 1855–1868* (Addis Ababa and Lund, 1994), 197–201. See also Markham, *Expedition,* 76–7.

ii-13.   *Correspondence,* 218–24.

ii-14.   On the earlier history of Ethiopia with European Christendom see Taddesse Tamrat, *Church and State in Ethiopia, 1270–1527* (Oxford, 1972).

ii-15.   *Correspondence,* 229, 243.

ii-16.   Ibid, 238–42.

ii-17.   The kosso tree, *Hagenia Abyssinica,* grows in the Abyssinian highlands. In rural areas, its flowers are still used to cure tapeworm.

ii-18   Dajazmach Kasa, the ruler of Tegray, subsequently became Emperor Yohannes IV. Tegray (or Tigré, Tigray) was the most northerly, and at this time probably the most powerful, of Ethiopia's Christian provinces. For his life see Zewde Gabre-Sellassie, *Yohannes IV of Ethiopia: A Political Biography* (Oxford, 1975) and Bairu Tafla (ed.), A Chronicle of Emperor Yohannes IV (1872-89) (Weisbaden 1977).

      The title of *Dajazmach* or Dejasmatch was equivalent to Prince, but literally means "Warrior at the Gate" from *deja,* a door or gate. Prince Alamayou, son of Theodore, used the title of Dajazmach; so did the principal provincial officials, like Kasa.

      Simpson points out that both St. Peter and the Christian Pope are shown with keys, and the spiritual head of the Mohammedan world is known as "The Sublime Porte" ("Jottings," 608).

ii-19   Wagshum Gobazé Gabra Madhen was the hereditary ruler of Lasta. The district of Lasta, in which the rock churches of Lalibala are situated, was located some fifty miles north–north-east of Magdala.

ii-20.   Markham, *History,* 320–2.

ii-21.   Ibid, 327.

ii-22.   Ibid, 330–1.

ii-23.   Blanc, *Narrative,* 406.

ii-24.   Markham, *History,* 340–1.

ii-25.   House of Commons, *Further Papers connected with the Abyssinian Expedition* (London, 1868), 6. See also Napier's subsequent speech at Westpool, quoted in *Theodore's Cattle* [author unknown], (Poona, 1869), 1.

ii-26.   Markham, *History,* 342–6.

ii-27.   Ibid, 351–2.

ii-28.   Ibid, 353.

ii-29.   On the looting of Magdala, the subsequent diffusion of looted manuscripts, and their influence on European scholarship see Rita Pankhurst, "The Library of Emperor Tewodros II at Maqdala (Magdala)," *Bulletin of the School of Oriental and African Studies* 36 (1973): 15–42; also the Memorandum from the Association for the Return of Maqdala Ethiopian Treasures (AFROMET), House of Commons, Culture, Media and Sport Committee, Seventh Report on Cultural Property: Return and Illicit Trade, Vol. 3 (London, 2000), 354–358.

ii-30.   [Yohannes Kotziga] "Methodios, Metropolitan of Aksum: An Unpublished document edited and translated into English," *Abba Salama,* 1 (1970): 51.

ii-31   Theophilus Waldmeier, *The Autobiography of Theophilus Waldmeier, Missionary* (London, 1886), 73–4.

ii-32.   Henry Dufton, *Narrative,* 105, 106.

ii-33.   Hormuzd Rassam, *Narrative of the British Mission to Theodore, King of Abyssinia* (London, 1869), 103–4.
          Rassam (1826–1910) was a Nestorian Christian from Turkey, who as a youth had been converted to Protestantism. Having assisted the British explorer Austin Layard in his famous investigations at Nineveh, he held official British posts in Aden and Zanzibar, and was chosen, in 1864, to take a letter from Queen Victoria to Emperor Tewodros, by whom he was later imprisoned. For more details, see also his Narrative, and Markham, History, 431 (index); and for his mission, as reported by an anonymous contemporary Ethiopian chronicler, L. Fusella, "La cronaca dell'Imperatore Teodoro II di Etiopia in un manoscritto amarico," *Annali dell' Instituto Universitario Orientale di Napoli* 6 (1954–6), 101–4.

ii-34.   Richard Pankhurst, "Captain Speedy's 'Entertainment;' The Reminiscences of a Nineteenth Century British Traveller to Ethiopia," *Africa,* 38 no. 3 (1983): 433.

ii-35.   Markham, *Expedition,* 293.

ii-36.   Alan Moorhead, *The Blue Nile* (New York), 205–6.

ii-37.   Sven Rubenson, *King of Kings,* 46.

ii-38.   ibid, 91.

ii-39   Donald Crummey, "The Violence of Téwodros," *Journal of Ethiopian Studies,* 9 no. 2 (1971): 107, 124–5. For examples of Téwodros' violence see also Luigi Fusella, "La Cronaca dell' Imperatore Teodoro II di Etiopia in un manoscritto amarico," *Annali dell' Instituto Universitario Orientale di Napoli,* 6 (1954–6): 107–9; Waldmeier, *Autobiography,* 93–6; Blanc, *Captivity,* 311–12, 315, 353–4.

ii-40.   Bahru Zedwe, *A History of Modern Ethiopia 1855–1974* (London, 1991), 27.

ii-41.   Tsegaye Gabre Medhin, "Tewodros. A Play," in *Ethiopian Observer,* 9 (1965): 209–226.

ii-42.   Richard Pankhurst, "Tsegaye Gabre Medhin's Opening Talk and Recitation," in Tadesse Beyene, Richard Pankhurst and Shiferaw Bekele, *Kasa and Kasa,* 5.

INTRODUCTION: WILLIAM SIMPSON (PAGES 26-37)

iii-1.   Letter to General Sir Thomas Biddulph, K.C.B., 2 March 1868. From Royal Archives, Windsor (RA PP Vic 1594 1868). Reproduced here by the gracious permission of Her Majesty The Queen.

iii-2.   Simpson provided a detailed account of his life in *The Autobiography of William Simpson, RI,* edited by G. Eyre-Todd (London, 1903). See also *Mr. William Simpson of the Illustrated London News: Pioneer War Artist 1823–1899* (London, 1987); *Dictionary of National Biography* (Supplement 22, 1973), 1217–1219; and A. H. H. Lipscomb (great-grandson of Simpson), "William Simpson (1823–1899), 'Prince of Pictorial Correspondents,'" (1999). Many additional articles on his life exist but these are the principal accounts used here.

iii-3.   William Simpson, "Notes and Recollections of my Life." 1892; referred to as: "Notes."

iii-4.   Simpson described some of his experiences in two articles published in the 1890s: "In the trenches before Sebastopol," in *English Illustrated Magazine,* 14 (December 1895); and "Winter and Summer in the trenches before Sebastopol," in *English Illustrated Magazine,* 15 (April 1896): 33–42. See also Peter Harrington, "The first true war artist," *MHQ, The Quarterly Journal of Military History,* 9 no. 1 (Autumn 1996): 100–109.

iii-5.   There was talk about purchasing the complete set of his original pictures for the nation, and letters vouching for their authenticity and artistic merit were sent by many of the leading commanders of the army, as well as other important artists. However the idea was voted down in Parliament, partly because they had already been engraved. *The Times,* 7 June 1856.

iii-6.   For details about Simpson's time in the Indian sub-continent and Tibet, see Mildred Archer and Paul Theroux, *Visions of India: The Sketchbooks of William Simpson, 1859–1862* (London, 1988).

iii-7.   An example is the watercolour by Simpson depicting the newly-opened Sudbury Practical Military College in Surrey which was reproduced in the *ILN* in 1857. The original is now in the Anne S. K. Brown Military Collection, Brown University Library. A variation of this image was published as a lithograph by Day and Son on 12 June 1857.

iii-8.   For example: "Artist's jottings in Abyssinia," *Good Words,* (1 October 1868): 605–613; "Church Architecture of Abyssinia," *Transactions of the Royal Institute of*

*British Architects, (*1873): 234–246.

iii-9.   Letter dated 6 November 1868. Royal Archives, Windsor (RA PP Vic 3303 1868). Reproduced here by the gracious permission of Her Majesty The Queen.

iii-10.   Hand-written endorsement on preceding note. Reproduced here by the gracious permission of Her Majesty The Queen.

iii-11.   Letter dated 30 November, 1868. Royal Archives, Windsor (RA PP Vic 3303 1863). Reproduced here by the gracious permission of Her Majesty The Queen.

iii-12.   William Simpson, *Autobiography*, 242–243.

iii-13.   Entry for 25 June 1879 in Simpson's diary for the war in Afghanistan. In the Anne S. K. Brown Military Collection, Brown University Library.

iii-14.   *Catalogue of Exhibition of War Sketches by the late William Simpson, R.I., R.B.A., F.R.G.S. "Illustrated London News" At Graves' Galleries, 6, Pall Mall, S.W.* (1900), page 7.

PART I: 3 March to 25 March, 1868 (PAGES 41-45)

1-1.   Marcus Keane was a popular Irish writer on architecture, who had recently published *The Towers and Temples of Ireland* (London, 1865).

1-2.   The port of Marseille was used by the steamers of the Peninsula and Orient (known as the P & O Line), the leading company sailing between Britain and the East.

1-3.   Lt. Col. Henry W. Parish —see Appendix C.
      Simpson also carried letters of introduction from two influential personalities, the Duke of Cambridge and Prince Edward of Saxe-Weimar (later King Edward VII).

1-4.   Reference is made to three places in the sacred city of Mecca: the al-Haram mosque; the Kaaba, or chief shrine, shaped in the form of a small, cube-like, windowless building; and Zamzam, the name of a sacred well.

1-5.   Judge Cursetjee, properly Cursetjee Manockjee Cursetjee (1847–1935). He was the first Indian to be admitted to Oxford as an undergraduate (in 1864). When Simpson met him he had been appointed as a judge in Bombay.

1-6.   The railroad linking Cairo to Suez (150 miles) was completed in 1857. Suez was a base for the Suez Canal Company and was therefore a large, crowded, and busy place at the time of Simpson's visit. The Canal opened for traffic on 17 November 1869, although not totally completed.

1-7.   * Identifies the first mention of British officers in the narrative—see Appendix C for more information on them.

1-8   Annesley Bay was situated on the Red Sea coast of Africa, some 70 miles south-east of the port of Massawa; it was the Expedition's place of disembarkation. The bay was named early in the nineteenth century by the British traveller Henry

Salt, who called it after his employer George Annesley, Viscount Valentia, who first saw it on 19 May 1804.

1-9.   The *Koina* was an iron, screw-driven ship, 706 tons, registered in Bombay.

1-10.   The *Sam Cearns* (also known as *Sam Cairns*) was carrying 350 tons of Commissariat stores for the Expedition.

1-11.   Shadwan, an island at the mouth of the Gulf of Suez, immediately north of the Red Sea.

1-12.   These islands were located in the northern Red Sea, nearly opposite the Egyptian port of Qusair.

1-13.   Sidees or Seedies, an Anglo-Indian term given to African immigrants to India, many of whom served as sailors.

1-14.   Napier, it should be recalled, had landed at the port of Annesley Bay on 2 January, had crossed the northern province of Tegray, and was less than three weeks' journey from his final destination, Magdala.

PART II: March to 5 April, 1868 (PAGES 47-60)

2-1.   Balaclava was one of the principal battles of the Crimean War. Simpson had been there as a war artist, and had later documented the campaign in his *Illustrations of the War in the East* (London, 1855–6).

2-2.   It is now generally agreed that this church was not Greek, but Aksumite. See D. W. Phillipson, *Ancient Ethiopia—Aksum: Its Antecedents and Successors* (London, 1998), 117–18.

2-3.   The Shoho (or more properly Saho), a nomadic Muslim people who ranged with their flocks between the Ethiopian mountains and the coast. These tribesmen levied taxes on merchants and others travelling through the commercially important area they controlled. Markham, *History,* 150–3, 385.

2-4.   The railway built by the Expedition ran from Annesley Bay through the torrid coastal lowlands to Koomaylee. For details on the line see Shepherd, *Campaign,* 39–40; H & H, *Record,* 507 (index); and, for a sketch map showing its route, D. G. Chandler, "The Expedition to Abyssinia, 1867–8" in B. Bond, *Victorian Military Campaigns,* 126.

2-5   At the end of the campaign, Chamberlain took an Ethiopian waif back to India with him, believing (incorrectly) that the lad was an orphan. He gave him his own Christian name of Charles and paid for his education. Charles Workneh Martin, as he was later known, became the first modern medical doctor in Ethiopia, and later served as the country's Minister to Britain [from *Ethiopia Observer,* 6 (1962), 251-3.]

2-6.   The Christian highlanders who lived near the coast apparently had a smattering of Arabic, and doubtless assumed that it was known to members of the Expedition. The word "tayib" was also the useful equivalent of the Mediterranean colloquial "Esta bene," signifying that either the object(s) sold, or the price, was good; or else that the latter had been agreed upon.

2-7.   A silk cord, known as a *matab*, was traditionally worn around the neck by Ethiopian Christians.

2-8.   Stanley (*Coomassie and Magdala*, 296), states that the pass was the "most difficult" part of the road, for the traveller had to pass through "a very narrow defile" flanked by "walls of sheet granite soaring up in all majesty to a height of 800 feet on each side." Colonel Milward commented that the pass was "worth having come from England to see." In Stanislaw Chojnacki and Innes Marshall, "Colonel Milward's Abyssinian Journal, 2 December 1867 to 13 June 1868," *Journal of Ethiopian Studies*, 7 no. 1 (1969): 92.

2-9.   Macadam, a technique of layering stone road coverings designed by the British road-builder John L. McAdam (1756–1836); and kunkur, a coarse limestone used for road-compacting in India. Henry Yule and A. C. Burnell, *Hobson-Jobson* (Calcutta, 1886), 496.

2-10.   "Devil's Staircase." This part of the road was constructed by two Indian contingents: the 10th Native Infantry and the Bombay Sappers. (Markham, *History*, 161, 163.)

2-11.   Undel Wells was described as "beyond question the most pleasant depôt in the pass, well watered, well sheltered, and possessing an agreeable climate." (Shepherd, *Campaign*, 54.)

2-12.   For more information on Hormuzd Rassam, see Note ii-33.
        The reference is to Maria Theresa dollars, or thalers, the only currency then in circulation in Ethiopia. Richard Pankhurst, *Economic History of Ethiopia 1800–1935* (Addis Ababa, 1968), 468–73. Rassam says that Téwodros gave him two monetary gifts, each of 5,000 Maria Theresa dollars (*Narrative*, I, 305, II, 45).

2-13.   The village of Goun-Gouna, 12 miles from Senafe, was said by Markham to have been "entirely deserted, owing to the depredations and excesses" of Hagos, a "robber chief" then in rebellion against Dajazmach Kasa, the ruler of Tegray (*History*, 197).

2-14.   Simpson's view of the origin of the name "Abyssinia" would not be accepted by modern scholars. The conventional view is that the word was derived from *Habashat*, the name of a people living near the Red Sea coast, who were the first inhabitants of the area with whom the Arabs became familiar. Edward Ullendorff, *The Ethiopians, An Introduction to Country and People* (London, 1960), 48. The word Ethiopia came from the Greek for "burnt faces," and was used by the Greeks to refer to the dark-skinned people south of Egypt; and when the Ethiopians adopted Christianity in the early fourth century they found the word Ethiopia in the Greek bible. Later, Europeans who learned of the country through the Arabs used Abyssinia/Abyssinie/Abissinia, while those who learned of it through the Greeks called it Ethiopia.
        The people of what we now call Ethiopia did not like the designation Habash or Abyssinian because they thought, probably wrongly, that it meant *Habash*, or "mixed." In modern times, the rest of the world has accepted the local preference for Ethiopia.

2-15.   Famines were not infrequent in Ethiopia. For their history see Richard Pankhurst, *The History of Famine and Epidemics in Ethiopia Prior to the Twentieth Century* (Addis Ababa, 1985).

2-16.   Irrigation was fairly well known but not extensively practiced in Ethiopia. Ibid, 187.

2-17.   The church of Dabra Libanos was situated halfway up a cliff overlooking Goun-Gouna, on a ledge not more than four to six feet wide. The Expedition seems to have known of this ecclesiastical establishment before arriving there, as they presented its clergy with an embroidered silk vestment bearing the words: "Presented to the Church of Abuna Libanos, Goun-Gouna, by His Excellency Sir Robert Napier, Commander-in-Chief, Abyssinian Field Force, 5th. February 1868." (Markham, *History,* 197; Shepherd, *Campaign,* 70.)

2-18.   Adigerat was the site, according to Markham, of "a few houses and many ruins, clustering around a church and ruined palace erected by the early nineteenth century ruler of Tegray, Dajazmach Sabagadis." In *History,* 199, 220, 229–30, 261. The settlement was described by Shepherd (*Campaign,* 72), as "a miserable collection of hovels, scarcely deserving the name of village."

2-19.   Adowa (or Adwa), the most important market town in Tegray. See *History of Ethiopian Towns from the Middle Ages to the Early Nineteenth Century* (Stuttgart, 1985), 89–107.

2-20.   The Expedition had a battery of four Armstrong guns which were transported by elephants. H & H, *Record,* I, 260; Myatt, *March,* 65.

2-21.   The church of Abuna Aragawi, called after one of the Nine Saints of that name, from Syria. He is believed to have arrived in Ethiopia in the late fifth or early sixth century. *Guida d'Italia della Consociazione Turistica Italiana,* Africa Orientale Italiana (Milan, 1938), 299. This church was described by Shepherd, *Campaign,* 73–4, as a "by no means inconsiderable building." It was, he thought, "a more recent structure" than the churches of Goun-Gouna or Focada, and was "much more elaborately decorated." Its paintings depicted Scriptural scenes from the Old and New Testaments, including the Pharaoh drowning in the Red Sea, and others illustrating "Abyssinian mythology." Shepherd goes on to claim that the "perspective and design of many of the representations" proved that the artist, who came from Debra Tabor, "was no mere amateur, but must have made a study of his trade." For further descriptions of these paintings see Stanley, *Coomassie and Magdala,* 313.

2-22.   The story of this "princess" and the identity of her husband are reported differently by different writers.

Both H & H, *Record,* I, 391, and Colonel Milward (Chojnacki and Marshall, "Journal," 93) state that the prisoner was a captive, not of Kasa, the ruler of Tegray, but of Wagshum Gobazé of Lasta. The official report adds that she "was said to pine away her life in incessant grief and pinching poverty."

Shepherd (*History,* 73), on the other hand, suggests that her husband was a prisoner of Téwodros, and that the "high-born and disconsolate lady who occupied the castle tower alone was likely soon to have her husband restored to her." Stanley,

Coomassie and Magdala, 312, likewise gives the impression that the husband was one of the Emperor's prisoners, for he claims that the British released him from his captivity at Magdala.

2-23.   The Expedition made extensive use of mules, large numbers of which perished on the journey to and from Magdala. 17,940 mules (and ponies) were originally landed at Annesley Bay, but only 4,126 were embarked at the end of the campaign. It was officially stated that no fewer than 3,225 mules died in the first four months of 1868 alone. H & H, *Record,* II, 234, 264–5.

2-24.   Bethelem [or Beateléhem, Beatalehem, Betleem house] meaning "House of Bread." Name for the hut or compartment in which priests baked the bread used in the Communion Service. For a description of the arrangement of a typical Ethiopian church see Henry Middleton Hyatt, *The Church of Abyssinia* (London, 1928), 109–30, 124.

2-25.   The term Abun (or Abuna)—literally, Father—was given to the head of the Ethiopian church.
         The reference is to the Coptic prelate Abuna Qérelos (1815–c. 1828). Though Simpson's allegations against him may not be fully substantiated, he was widely reputed to have been a drunkard, as well as venal and corrupt. Nathaniel Pearce, *The Life and Adventures of Nathaniel Pearce* (London, 1831), II, 55–6, 65–6; David Appleyard and Arthur Kinlock Irvine, *Letters from Ethiopian Rulers: Early and Mid-Nineteenth Century* (London, 1985), 46–51.

PART III: 6 April to 10 April (PAGES 61-71)

3-1.   Hauptmann (Captain) Theodor von Kodolitsch, attaché of the Austrian army. Kodolitsch subsequently wrote a series of articles on the Expedition.

3-2.   Thebaid, a word originally pertaining to Thebes; by extension, Egyptian; in this context, Coptic. On the character and significance of Ethiopian caves, see Richard Pankhurst, "Caves in Ethiopian History: Cave Sites in the Environs of Addis Ababa," *Ethiopia Observer* 16 (1973): 15–34.

3-3.   Capt. (Count) von Kielmansegge was an Austrian marine attaché.

3-4.   Reference is made to the Mexican Revolution of 1867, led by Benito Juarez, in the course of which the Emperor Maximilian was executed by the rebels.

3-5.   The Gallas—now more frequently referred to as Oromo—belonged to an ethnic group once living in southern Ethiopia who, in the sixteenth century, began advancing into the central areas of the country, as far north as the borders of Tegray.

3-6.   Match-lock weapons were by that time largely obsolete. On the introduction and diffusion of such weapons see Richard Pankhurst, "Linguistic and Cultural Data on the Penetration of Fire-arms into Ethiopia," *Journal of Ethiopian Studies*, 9 no 1 (1971): 47–82.

3-7.   Lokomo, Tigrinya, an archaic term for roasted grain or chick-peas eaten by Tegray peasants and others as a kind of snack. We are indebted to Dr Hailu Araya, formerly of Addis Ababa University, for this identification.

3-8.   Cowrie shells were imported from the Red Sea, and also used in necklaces. See Pankhurst, *Economic History of Ethiopia,* 356, 438, 445.

3-9.   Agriculture in the Ethiopian highlands was based primarily on a simple iron-tipped wooden plough pulled by two oxen. Pankhurst, ibid, 185–7.

3-10.   Orissa, a province in north-west India, was the site of several major famines.

3-11.   A plan of this church is reproduced in Markham, *History,* between 236 and 237. The modern archaeologist David Phillipson describes it as "a rectangular structure on a massive plinth" of typically Aksumite design. Phillipson, *Ancient Ethiopia, 117–18.*

3-12.   Antalo had been the capital, in the early nineteenth century, of Ras Walda Sellasé, ruler of Tegray. By the time the Expedition passed through the town, the palace building was, according to Markham, "an utter ruin." Shepherd nevertheless believed that the settlement had previously been "a large town," though by then "about two-thirds" were in ruins. Though the town, as Markham agrees, was "ruined and decayed;" there was, he states, "still a great weekly market" to which people came "from miles around." There were moreover eight churches in the vicinity of the town, "each with its pleasant grove of trees." Markham, *History,* 238–9; Shepherd, *Campaign,* 139; H & H, *Record,* II, 72, 488 (index).

PART IV: 11 April TO 15 April (Pages 72-79)

4-1.   Shepherd, op. cit. 172, reports seeing "luxuriant vegetation—giant junipers....trees of heather (*erica arborea*) in full and profuse bloom, St. John's wort all a blaze of yellow, myrtles, acacias, and varieties of sweet pea." *Rosa abyssinica* was known in Amharic as *qeg* or *tsigé.* Wolde Michael Kelecha, *Glossary,* 84, 228.

4-2.   *Carduus ellenbeckii,* known in Amharic as *ya-ahiya isohohi.* Wolde Michael Kelecha, op. cit., 23, 188.

4-3.   An allusion to Tacitus' *Agricola,* where Calcagus, referring to the Romans, observes, "where they made a desert, they call it peace."

4-4.   Roderick Dhu was a Scottish chieftain who appears as a character in Walter Scott's *Marmion* and other novels.

4-5.   "Sultan," Arabic for a ruler, generally of a Muslim state; "Sahib," an Anglo-Indian honorific applied to Europeans.

4-6.   Dugald Dalgetty (or Dalgety) was a character in Walter Scott's novel *A Legend of the Wars of Montrose.*

4-7.   In fact *talaab* [Hindustani], a small pond.

4-8.   Butter was widely used as a hair-oil, by both men and women. Richard Pankhurst, *A Social History of Ethiopia* (Addis Ababa, 1990), 72, 154.

4-9.   Probably the fleshy fruit of the *Citrus grandis,* known in Amharic as *terengo.* Wolde Michael Kelecha, *Glossary,* 128.

4-10.   *Hambasha,* circular bread, often eaten on special occasions.

4-11.   Markham, *History,* 311, records that on 8 April two brigades reached the Dalanta plateau, "in full view of the Magdala heights."

Part V: 16 April to 20 April (PAGES 80-91)

5-1.   For an official list of the European captives liberated see H & H, *Record,* II, 48–9. For their Ethiopian designations, see Luigi Fusella, "Cronaca," 115–117.

5-2.   Fitawrawi Gabriyé, the commander of Téwodros' advance-guard. Described by Markham as "a gallant old General," with "many grey hairs," he was "said to have been as good as he was brave....Ever foremost in the fight [against the British, he] returned again and again to the charge with great bravery," but was "killed by a Snider rifle-bullet through his temples." He was found "lying flat on his back, with his arms stretched out...dressed in a rich shirt of crimson silk and gold. His horse was lying dead about ten paces from him." Markham, *History,* 321, 328. See also Rassam, *Mission,* II, 276; Shepherd, *Campaign,* 245; Myatt, *March,* 137, 140, 144, 147, 149, 154; Bates, *Abyssinian Difficulty,* 183, 190–1.

5-3.   As shown in Richard Pankhurst's introduction to this account, Napier explained his position on Tewodros in his first report after the capture of Magdala. Writing to the Secretary of State for India on 14 April, he declared it "essential for the vindication of our national honour, which he has so grossly insulted, that he should be removed for ever from his place." House of Commons, *Further Papers,* 6. On the correspondence between the British commander and the Emperor see also David Appleyard and Richard Pankhurst, "The Last Two Letters of Emperor Tewodros II of Ethiopia (April 11 and 12 1868," *Journal of the Royal Asiatic Society,* 1 (1986): 23–32.

5-4.   The Snider Rifle was a new weapon, here used in warfare by the British for the first time. Simpson was pointing out the number of shells it could fire in only a few hours.

5-5.   Napier in fact sent only one letter to Tewodros. Written on 11 April 1868, it called on the Emperor to "submit to the Queen of England," and promised "honourable treatment." In Napier's words,

> Your Majesty has fought like a brave man, and has been overcome by the superior power of the British Army. It is my desire that no more blood may be shed. If, therefore, your Majesty will submit to the Queen of England, and bring all the Europeans now in your Majesty's hands, and deliver them safely this day in the British camp, I guarantee honourable treatment for yourself and all members of your Majesty's family. (House of Commons, *Further Papers,* 8.)

5-6.   The Wadela Plain was described by Markham, *History,* 254, 282–4, as "a mighty wall, rising abruptly" from the nearby plains, while Shepherd, *Campaign,* 204, observed the area was windswept, and added: "Not a single tree or bush is visible upon its whole expanse to afford shade from the burning sun by day, and shelter from the piercing wind by night."

5-7.   The man was probably using the Amharic word *saffar,* for "camp." Thomas Lieper Kane, *Amharic-English Dictionary* (Weisbaden, 1990), I, 593.

5-8.   Reference is made to the Land of Goshen, the country to which Joseph and the Israelite shepherds migrated in Biblical times. Gen. 46:28–34.

5-9.   The Dalanta plain was a nearly flat area formed of columnar basalt. According to Markham, *History,* 284–5, it was covered with "grass and ploughed land, but quite treeless" except for clumps of trees around the churches.

5-10.   Tewodros' road impressed all observers. Stanley, *Coomassie and Magdala,* 397, claims that the Emperor in making it "worked as hard as any of his men," while Shepherd, *Campaign,* 217, declares that the road "bore witness to the perseverance and pains-taking of its maker."

5-11.   Simpson arrived too late to witness the Victory Parade, which was held on the morning of 20 April on the Dalanta Plain.

5-12.   Lieutenant Count (Graf) von Seckendorff, Prussian attaché. *Meine Erlebnisse mit dem englischen Expeditionscorps in Abessinien, 1867–1868* (Potsdam, 1869).

5-13.   Henry Morton Stanley (1841–1904), author and journalist, whose real name was John Rowlands. Today he is best known for finding the missionary David Livingstone. He accompanied the Expedition and described his experiences in *Coomassie and Magdala* (London, 1874).

5-14.   Dajazmach Alamayou (1861–1879), the Queen's son by Téwodros, was later taken to England. See Basil William Sholto Mackenzie, Lord Amulree, "Prince Alamayou of Ethiopia," *Ethiopia Observer* 13 (1970): 8–15; Darrell Bates, "The Abyssinian Boy," *History Today* (December 1979), 816–23. See also C[ornelia] C[otton], i.e., Mrs. Speedy, *Anecdotes of Almayu, the Late King Theodore's Son* (London, n.d.). See also Part X. The literal meaning of the name Alamayou, according to Simpson, is *"He has seen the world,* a name which seems to have been curiously prophetic in its import." ("Jottings," 608)

5-15.   Stanley, *Coomassie and Magdala,* 470–1.

5-16.   Rassam, *Mission,* II, 44–5. See also Henry Aaron Stern, *The Captive Missionary* (London, 1868), 256–9; F. Gibbs, "Account of the Order of the Cross and Seal of Solomon proposed to have been founded by King Theodore of Abyssinia," *Proceedings of the Bombay Branch of the Royal Asiatic Society* (1889) and, on Zander, see Fusella, "Cronaca," 116.

5-17.   *Toshaconna,* Anglo-Indian: the repository for safekeeping of articles received as presents, or intended as such.

5-18.   Mashasha, Téwodros' eldest son. Born around 1840, he had for a time been governor of Dambeya. Rassam, *Mission,* II, 45, 57–8, 336; Sven Rubenson, *King of Kings,* 56.

        Ras Ingada, or Ingida, was one of Tewodros' most loyal courtiers. Rassam believed that the chief would have "swallowed a drought of deadly poison...out of deference to what he considered his bounden duty to his sovereign," and adds: "during the last four years of the King's reign, he never slept a night in his own house, but in a tent or a miserable hut, within call both by day and night." Ingada, he adds, "hated gossip; and its kindred vices of mischief-making and back-biting," and "eschewed all intoxicating drinks and a plurality of wives, and held those in disesteem who indulged in them." Despite his loyalty the chief subsequently fell into disgrace. He was imprisoned at Magdala, and put in chains, but was later released, and, ever faithful to his master, died during the final British assault on the citadel, on 13 April 1868. Rassam, *Mission,* I, 255–8, 261, 277; Rubenson, *Tewodros,* 53, 75.

The title of *Ras* is also used in Arabic, according to Simpson ("Jottings," 608). According to Kane's *Dictionary* (I, 381), it means "head" in Amharic and denotes a rank immediately below that of *Negus,* or king.

5-19.   Dr Henry Blanc: a medical officer at Aden, who was appointed to the Rassam Mission. On his life, and detention, see his Narrative of Captivity in Abyssinia; also Rassam, *Mission,* I, 2; Arnold, *Prelude,* 331 (index).

Ras Tagga: Téwodros' Commander-in-Chief, who was in charge of the riflemen. Toward the end of the reign he fell into disgrace, was imprisoned, and chained at Magdala, but was later released. Rassam, *Mission,* II, 45, 277.

Ras Wald Mariam: This is conceivably a reference to a chief of that name who had earlier been appointed by Téwodros to supervise the transportation of the British mission's baggage. Rassam, who mentions this individual, does not, however, indicate that the man ever held the exalted title of Ras. Rassam, *Mission,* II, 196.

Ras Gabrei (or Gabre): another of the important courtiers of this time, whom Téwodros imprisoned at Magdala, but released immediately prior to the British assault. Rassam, *Mission,* II, 261.

5-20.   Astronomy had its adherents in Ethiopia. For example—according to Henry Blanc, Téwodros' chief scribe, Alaqa Zanab, was "quite mad on astronomy, and would listen for hours to anything concerning the solar system." Blanc, *Captivity,* 219. Interest in astronomy extended into astrology, on which see Otto Neugebauer, *Ethiopic Astronomy and Computus* (Vienna, 1979), 19–21, 183–4, 201.

5-21.   *Ya Solomon,* Amharic, literally, ya, 'of' Solomon; *Mahtam,* Amharic, literally, a seal, or stamp; *Masqal,* Amharic, a cross, or *masqalu,* the cross (Kane, *Dictionary.*)

Rassam (*Narrative* 1, 22–5) stated that Téwodros, wishing to honour the British diplomatic mission, summoned four Ethiopian goldsmiths and asked Rassam to advise them how to make the required medals. However he was not satisfied with their work and ordered that it should be carried out by a German, Christophe Zander, one of the missionary craftsmen at his court. A schematic representation of the resultant insignia is given in Rassam's *Narrative,* which indicates that the motto on the obverse should read, presumably in Ge'ez, "Theodorus, King of kings of Ethiopia," and the reverse, "The fear of the Lord is the beginning of wisdom."

PART VI: 22 April to 5 May (PAGES 93-109)

6-1.   Queen Terunash (1842–1868), also referred to as Teruwarq, was the daughter of Dajazmach Webé Hayla Maryam of Samén and Tegra. She was Téwodros' second wife. She was reputedly only twelve at the time of her marriage. Markham, *History,* 72, 361–2, 280; Shepherd, *Campaign,* 264; Rassam, *Mission,* II. 217, 277, 336; Rubenson, *Tewodros,* 56.

6-2.   Exodus 15: 21. "Sing ye to the Lord, for he hath triumphed gloriously: the horse and his rider hath he thrown into the sea."

6-3.   Psalms, 47: 1. "O clap your hands, all ye people, shout unto God with the voice of triumph."

6-4.   Dajazmach Berru, the ruler of Gojjam (or Goggam), had been imprisoned by Téwodros. After the Emperor's death and the release of his Ethiopian prisoners, Berru made his way to his own country—a large Christian province in north-west Ethiopia which was circumscribed to the north, east and south by the great bend of the Abbay, or Blue Nile.

6-5.   Lieutenant Morgan, of the Royal Engineers, was described by Markham as "a most zealous and promising young officer, beloved and respected by his men, and always sharing the toils of the weary marches with them instead of riding the horse to which he was entitled." Morgan's death, according to Shepherd, was the result of "brain fever," induced by "over application to the responsible and arduous duties" imposed on him. (Markham, *History,* 219, 372; Shepherd, *Campaign,* 210, 293–4. See also Stanley, *Coomassie and Magdala,* 485; and H & H, *Record,* II, 80.)

6-6.   King Lalibala (c.1182–c.1225), one of the principal rulers of the supposedly usurping Zagwé dynasty. Renowned as the builder of the famous monolithic rock-hewn churches at the holy city which bears his name, he was later canonised by the Ethiopian Orthodox Church.

6-7.   The Zagwé dynasty included the sixteen kings who ruled from around 920 to 1253. Sergew Hable Sellassie, *Ancient and Medieval Ethiopian History to 1270* (Addis Ababa, 1972), 239–87. However Simpson is here mistaken, in that the tradition to which he refers holds that the founder of the Zagwé dynasty was not a son of the Queen of Sheba by someone other than Solomon, but was Solomon's son by one of the Queen of Sheba's slave-girls. Ibid, 241.

6-8.   See Note 2-24.

6-9.   The Baobab, or *Adansonoa digitata,* a tree with an extraordinarily wide trunk. Wolde Michael Kelecha, op cit., 197.

6-10.   The Expedition was accompanied by more than forty Indian elephants, which were used to transport supplies. They created considerable interest among the Ethiopian population. Stanley declared that these beasts, who were fed 35 pounds of bread and 40 pounds of straw a day, were "at once the terror and the delight of the natives who crowded around them...[who] seemed never tired of watching their uncouth and unwieldy forms ascending or descending mountains." Forty-four elephants were landed at Annesley Bay at the beginning of the campaign; five died and the survivors were shipped back at the conclusion of operations. H & H, *Record,* II, 495 (index).

6-11.   The first Biblical texts in Amharic had been printed by the British and Foreign Bible Society in London in 1824, and the first complete Amharic-language Bible appeared in 1840. G. E. Coldham, *A Bibliography of Scriptures in African Languages* (London, 1966), 10, 12. Ethiopian Biblical and other manuscripts, for the most part in Ge'ez, were written on parchment made of the skins of cattle, sheep, goats and even horses. For a description of the preparation of such volumes see Sergew Hable Sellassie, *Bookmaking in Ethiopia* (Leiden, 1981).

Ge'ez, also known as Ethiopic, has been termed the Latin of Ethiopia. Thought to have been spoken in and around Aksum (also spelled as Axum) in ancient times, it remained the language of the Ethiopian Orthodox Church: the language of the Bible and the liturgy, as well as classical Ethiopic literature. Ge'ez is likewise the root of a group of Ethiopian Semitic languages, which include Amharic and Tigrinya, the latter spoken in the north of the country. (Ullendorff, *Ethiopians*, 113–126.)

6-12.   Debra Tabor was the capital of Bagemder province, and site of Téwodros' earlier capital.

Contrary to Simpson's statement that Mahdara Kal had been imprisoned by Téwodros for "eight years," a subsequent British traveller reports that he served the Ethiopian monarch up to the latter's death, and "appeared to entertain a sincere affection for his old master." Emelius Albert De Cosson, *The Cradle of the Blue Nile: A Visit to the Court of King John of Ethiopia* (London, 1877), II, 52–5.

Mahdara Kal (or Qal) was born in the northern province of Tegray and taken to Paris as a youth by the French traveller Théophile Lefebvre, who published the young man's portrait in his *Voyage en Abyssinie* 6 (Paris, 1845–1848). He was subsequently enrolled at the Jesuit Collège Henri IV, after which he moved to a Protestant College in Malta, and later to Mr. Leider's Church of England missionary establishment in Cairo. On returning to his native country, in about 1865, he joined Téwodros' service as a translator. He interpreted between the Emperor and the French envoy, who reported, however, that Téwodros did not like his young compatriot, and chose every opportunity to ridicule him. Guillaume Lejean, *Voyage en Abyssinie executé de 1862 à 1864* (Paris, 1872), 10. See also Taddese Beyene, Pankhurst and Shiferaw Bekele, *Kasa and Kasa*, 258–9.

Captain Alexandre Girard, a subsequent French traveller, quoted Mahdara Kal (who had by then entered the service of Emperor Yohannes IV) as stating that Téwodros had made a mistake in "closing himself up" to fight the English at Magdala. If he had instead gone into the countryside and harassed his enemies, as Abd-el-Kader had done in Algeria, "not a single Englishman," Mahdara Kal declared, "would have escaped; all without exception would have found their grave in our river-beds." Alexandre Girard, *Souvenirs d'un voyage en Abyssinie (1868–9)* (Cairo, 1873), 195–6.

6-13.   Pauline Flad was the wife of the Protestant missionary Martin Flad; both had been Theodore's prisoners.

6-14.   See Richard Pankhurst's Introduction, notes ii-19 and ii-20.

6-15.   Faris Aly [Ali], a chieftain of Yejju. Released after Téwodros' death, he "departed at once," Markham recalls, "without even paying his respects to the English General," Robert Napier. Markham, *History,* 363–4. See also Zewde Gabre-Sellassie, *Yohannes,* 31; Rubenson, *Tewodros,* 44, 50.

6-16.   Dajazmach Meshasha Tadla, the maternal uncle and deputy of the ruler of Lasta, Wagshum Gobazé. On 29 March, a fortnight before the Battle of Magdala, Meshasha visited the British camp, on the latter's behalf, stating that he had "his master's orders to render all his assistance in his power," and later supplied the

Expedition with a considerable quantity of provisions. He is described by Markham as "a dark man, rather beyond middle age, with very Jewish features, and a deep cut on his left check [sic] and ear. He had a sword with a handsomely-ornamented scabbard, and a splendid shield with bosses of filigree gold-work, and a lion's tail. His manners were quiet, dignified and very prepossessing."

After the battle of Magdala, the British proposed to hand over the fortress to him, on the Wagshum's behalf, but Meshasha, according to Markham, "after some consideration resolved to decline the proffered gift." This decision, Rubenson believes, was "most probably due" to the fact that Napier intended to destroy the Magdala arsenal, which would have left the fortress virtually undefendable. Meshasha, as Simpson notes, was subsequently captured by Faris Ali. Markham, *History,* 301–3, 306, 366, 371.

6-17.   Yejoo or Yeju, a district inhabited largely by Muslim Oromo. Situated south of Lasta and north of the Bashilo river, its hereditary ruler was Téwodros' first father-in-law, Ras Ali Alula.

6-18.   The Ethiopians had acquired a station at the Holy Sepulchre from Sultan Saladin of Jerusalem (1137–1193). On the long history of Ethiopian contacts with the Holy City, and of Ethiopian pilgrimage thereto, see Enrico Cerulli, *Etiopi in Palestina: Storia della comunità etiopica di Gerusalemme* (Rome 1946–1948).

The story of this monk is repeated in Simpson's *Autobiography,* 199–200.

6-19.   Present-day historians of Ethiopia would see Téwodros as requiring firearms not so much for the conquest of Jerusalem as for the subjection of his domestic enemies, and hence for the country's unification. Rubenson, *Survival,* 172–200, 205–77.

6-20.   See note ii-9 to Richard Pankhurst's Introduction, referring to casting of cannons by the Western craftsmen.

6-21.   Probably *Hypericum quartinianum,* known in Amharic as *amija.* Wolde Michael Kelecha, op cit., 56, 112.

6-22.   Simpson's figures, and dating, would appear inaccurate. Alaqa Berru, the Ethiopian envoy dispatched to fetch a new Abun, did not leave the port of Massawa until February of the following year (1869). He was entrusted with 20,000 Maria Theresa dollars, raised on the basis of a levy of two dollars per head of the tax-paying population around Aksum. The Abun, by name Atnatewos, left Egypt in June of that year. (Zewde Gabre-Sellassie, *Yohannes,* 34.)

6-23.   *Negusa Nagast,* Ge'ez and Amharic, literally "King of Kings," was often translated into English as Emperor.

6-24.   Menelik, son of King Solomon of Israel and the Ethiopian Queen of Sheba.

6-25.   This individual should not be confused with his near-contemporary Emperor Yohannes, the husband of Empress Manan. Rubenson, *Survival,* 90, 94, 88, 189.

6-26.   *Janhoy,* Amharic, i.e. "O Majesty!" or "His Majesty," a term used when addressing or referring to a monarch. Kane, *Dictionary,* II, 1897.

6-27.   The legend of Prester John, which was entirely without foundation, had circulated in Europe since the thirteenth century. The legend centered on a belief that somewhere in East there was a great Christian king whose overriding ambition was to help the West defeat the Saracens, and thus win Jerusalem for Christianity. Strenuous efforts were made to find this imaginary ruler, somewhere in the Indian region, but when these proved unsuccessful, belief in an Asian Prester John was replaced by the idea that the non-existent ruler was in fact the Christian emperor of Ethiopia, whose existence had by then been long attested. V. Slessarev, *Prester John. The Letter and the Legend* (Minneapolis, 1959); Wilhelm Baum, *Die Verwandlungen des Mythos vom Reich des Priestkönigs Johannes* (Flagenfurt, 1999).

PART VII: 6 May to 15 May (PAGES 110–118)

7-1.   Juniper, or cedar, *junipus procera,* known in Amharic as *tid.* Wolde Michael Kelecha, *Glossary,* 58, 201, 212.

7-2.   A tree commonly seen in the Ethiopian highlands. Wolde Michael Kelecha, ibid, 44, 208; Azene Bekele-Tesemma, *Useful Trees and Shrubs in Ethiopia* (Addis Ababa, 1993), 214–15.

7-3.   The rain that day was so heavy that Colonel Milward noted in his diary that "I never saw such rain since China....The ground was a puddle....It is to be hoped that we may not have many more such nights." Chojnacki and Marshall, "Journal," 111.

7-4.   The above authority was in fact as reliable as could be expected. For the typical rainfall pattern see Augustus Blande Wylde, *Modern Abyssinia* (London, 1901), 483.

7-5.   Amba Alaja, or Amba Alagi, a lofty mountain, with edges so steep that Shepherd comments: "it was almost impossible to believe that men and mules had descended its almost perpendicular sides in safety." Shepherd, *Campaign,* 169.

7-6.   Walda Yasus, a chief from the district of Wajerat (not Wogara, as Simpson notes), who was then struggling against Dajazmach Kasa of Tegray.
        Wogara, or Wagara, was a district some 50 miles north of Lake Tana.

7-7.   Shepherd, *Campaign,* reports, 311, that this pass was "twice..rendered utterly impassable." On the difficulties of the march at this time see also Stanley, *Coomassie and Magdala,* 495–7.

7-8   The battle of Arogee, a small plain half-way between the fortress of Magdala and the Bashilo river, was the first decisive engagement between Téwodros and the British, fought on 10 April 1868. For an account of the battle as seen by an observer on the Ethiopian side, see Waldmeier, *Autobiography,* 109–10.

7-9.   Waldubba, an important, largely inaccessible monastery near the Takazze river in Samén. Bairu Tafla, *Asma Giyorgis and His Work: History of the Galla and the Kingdom of Sawa* (Stuttgart, 1987), 984.

7-10.   Ethiopian monks claim to follow the rules of St. Anthony the hermit (d. 359 AD), who lived on Mount Kalzim near the north-west corner of the Red Sea. Hyatt, *Church,* 69.
        The *Echagé,* or head of the monks, was the second most important ecclesiastic in Ethiopia after the Abun, or Metropolitan; but, unlike the latter, was a native-born

Ethiopian. Hyatt, *Church,* 50–1.

7-11.　The two attachés were Brigadier Don Hipolito Llorante (in Shepherd, referred to as Florenti), and Lt.-Colonel (Count) de Mirasol.

7-12.　The crown, together with the chalice mentioned below, was duly purchased for the British Museum for £2,000, but only after heated debate in the House of Commons. In a discussion, on 30 June 1871, it was revealed that Lord Napier had given it as his opinion that the two artifacts should be deposited in the British Museum "until an opportunity offered for restoring them" to Abyssinia. Prime Minister William Ewart Gladstone went further. He declared that he "deeply regretted" that the two artifacts "were ever brought from Abyssinia, and could not conceive why they were so brought." Commenting on Napier's views on the return of the two articles, he observed that "if they ought to be returned, it seemed to follow that they should not have been brought from Abyssinia" in the first place. House of Commons, *Parliamentary Record* (1871), 939–50.

　　　For descriptions of the crown, chalice and other loot see also Stanley, *Coomassie and Magdala,* 458–9.

7-13.　Sir Richard Rivington Holmes (1835–1911), Assistant Curator at the British Museum, was appointed "Archaeologist" to the Expedition. In the course of his brief stay in Téwodros' erstwhile capital he acquired over 300 Ethiopic manuscripts for the Museum, besides the crown and chalice mentioned above.

> Holmes also purchased, on his own account, an important icon of the kwera'ata re'esu or Christ with the Crown of Thorns, which Ethiopian rulers had for centuries taken with them on campaign. The subsequent Ethiopian monarch, Emperor Johannes IV, wrote in 1872 appealing to Queen Victoria and to the British Foreign Secretary, Earl Granville, for the return of the painting. It could not, however, be found, and they wrote back that they "did not believe it had been taken to England." After the Emperor's death, however, Sir Richard, who was by then Librarian of the Royal Library in Windsor Castle, published a photograph of the painting in the *Burlington Magazine* of 1905, revealing that he had himself acquired the icon, and that it was in his personal possession. From Richard Pankhurst, "The History of an Ethiopian Icon," *African Affairs,* 81 (1982), 117–25.

Holmes, who was something of an artist, later served as Librarian of the Royal Library, Windsor Castle (from 1870 to 1906.) He also wrote lives of both Queen Victoria and her son Edward VII.

7-14.　This seal, which Simpson describes as noted above in his "Artist's Jottings," bore a crudely executed effigy of a Lion of Judah, standing on four paws, and wearing a crown surmounted by a cross. The inscription, the first to be written in Arabic as well as in Ge'ez, read: "King of Kings Tewodros of Ethiopia" (in Ge'ez), and "The Victorious King Tawudrus of Abyssinia" (in Arabic). The seal was deposited in London in the Victoria and Albert Museum, but was later returned to Ethiopia, when Queen Elizabeth presented it to Emperor Haile Sellassie I in Asmara in 1965.

7-15.   Chelicut had been the residence of an important earlier governor of Tegray, Ras Walda Sellasé, who ruled from 1790 until his death in 1816.

Markham, who in fact considered it a town, described it as "far and away the most pleasant and most picturesque" he had seen on the march. The streets were "narrow and stony....[but] all the houses [were] surrounded by gardens of chile pepper and groves of trees, with hedges of the shivi plant (*Pircunia Abyssinica*)." There were also "several plantain and one or two peach trees." Markham, *History,* 237–8.

7-16.   This edifice is also described by Markham, who states that it was "surrounded by superb juniper trees of great height," and adds:

> It is a circular edifice, with the wall of the outer cloister painted in the same style as that at Adigerat, with pictures of sacred objects and of the warlike deeds of the old Ras [Walda Sellasé]. The outer wall consists of a series of narrow arches, forming an arcade, those fronting the door into the Holy of Holies being filled in with a screen of carved woodwork. The general effect is certainly very pleasing. The roof is neatly thatched, and the doors and other woodwork are merely worked up with adzes, without the use of planes. Near these church two glorious dahro-trees spread a wide shade over a strip of soft turf, bordered by a running stream; and here the elders of the town meet to discuss their affairs. (Markham, *History,* 238.)

7-17.   Chelicut was visited in 1809 by the British envoy Henry Salt, who presented Ras Walda Sellasé with a number of presents. These gifts were deposited in the church, and Simpson probably saw them. They included a painted glass window, a painting of the Virgin Mary, and a "handsome" marble table. Henry Salt, *A Voyage to Abyssinia* (London, 1814), 266.

7-18.   *Alaqa,* Amharic, literally chief, a title given to the head of a church or monastery, or, as a sign of respect, to a person of traditional religious learning. Kane, *Dictionary,* II, 1107.

7-19.   Ethiopians, in fear of the Evil Eye, were traditionally reluctant to be seen eating or drinking. Walter Chichele Plowden, *Travels in Abyssinia and the Galla Country* (London, 1868), 124.

7-20   *Salaam,* Amharic; literally not "health," but "peace." Kane, *Dictionary,* I, 444.

7-21.   *Bét,* Amharic, a house. Kane, Dictionary, I, 911.

7-22.   On the history of these manuscripts, their distribution to churches on the "line of march," and their acquisition by British and other European libraries see Rita Pankhurst, "The library of Emperor Tewodros II at Mäqdäla (Magdala)," *Bulletin of the School of Oriental and African Studies,* 36 no. 1 (1973): 15–42.

PART VIII: 16 May to 24 May (PAGES 119-126)

8-1.   The Queen was "greatly beloved by all the people," Shepherd, Campaign, 324, says, "and many and genuine were the signs of grief displayed on account of her death." She was buried, according to Markham, *History,* 380, "beside the body of brave old Râs Walda Selassyè." See also Rassam, *Mission,* II, 347–8.

Simpson reports in the *Illustrated London News* (published 27 June) that she had been ill for some time with "pulmonary disease....It is the opinion of the surgeons that a rupture of some internal blood vessel was the immediate cause of her almost sudden death." Contrary to some parts of the preceding information, he stated that she was born "in January 1850 at Mai Sahlo, in the district of Samén. Her father was the Ras Oubieh, formerly Prince of Tegray, who was conquered by Theodore and kept a prisoner till he died. The Queen's proper name was Tiroowark, which means 'pure gold' but at her baptism she was called Walata Tekla Haimanout, or Daughter of Tekla Haimanout."

8-2   The Queen's supposed detention at Magdala is not mentioned in the writings of any of the European prisoners, or confirmed in any other source. It is presumably incorrect.

8-3.   It is interesting to note that the queen's mother, Wayzaro Laqiyaye, a noble-woman of Samén, endeavored to keep in contact with her grandson Prince Alamayou during his stay in England, and wrote both to him and to Queen Victoria about him. Appleyard and Irvine, *Letters,* 147–56.

8-4.   This church is described by Ruth Plant in *The Architecture of the Tigray, Ethiopia* (Worcester, 1985), 94–5, as "probably the greatest of all churches in the Tigray."

8-5.   These two rulers, whose names Simpson correctly translates, have been described by the modern historian Stuart Munro-Hay as "preeminent in Ethiopian tradition." They were "brothers who are said to have ruled jointly," and were "converted to Christianity in the early fourth century by the Syrian Frumentius," their example being "eventually followed by the entire nation." Stuart Munro-Hay, *Aksum: An African Civilisation of Late Antiquity* (Edinburgh, 1991), 13. See also Sergew Hable Sellassie, *Ancient History,* passim. See also note 8-6.

8-6.   Hiob Ludolf, *Nouvelle histoire d'Abissinie ou d'Ethiopie* (Paris, 1684), 94. (see also note 8-5.)

8-7.   In his *Autobiography,* Simpson tells the story somewhat differently. He suggests that Napier had at first planned that his party should make its way to the historic city of Aksum, but was prevented only by the proximity of the rains.

> It was Sir Robert Napier's intention to have made up a large party of all the foreign officers at Headquarters, and the correspondents, with whom he would have branched off somewhere about Adigerat, and paid a visit to Aksum, the ancient capital of Abyssinia, where certain obelisks and other remains of antiquity still exist. In the old church at that place is pre-served the real ark of the covenant which was carried off from Jerusalem by Menelik, the son of the Queen of Sheba. But the rainy season was close at hand. In fact, one heavy fall had taken place and carried off some men in the Sooroo Pass, and the Commander-in-Chief, fearing further danger, would not risk delay. So this expedition, much to my regret, was aban-doned. (*Autobiography,* 195.)

This picture of events is not, however, corroborated by a geologist who accompanied the Expedition. He states that Napier, after the capture of Magdala, "would not listen to any proposals of exploration...[and] was determined to have every European over whom he could in any way exercise authority out of the country in as short a time as possible." William T. Blandford, *Observations on the Geology and Zoology of Abyssinia* (London, 1870), 91–2.

8-8.　　For a scholarly modern account of Aksum and its famous obelisks, see Munro-Hay, *Aksum,* especially 104–43.

8-9.　　The obelisks bore no inscriptions; Simpson was here writing from hearsay. Such inscriptions as existed elsewhere in the city were written in Ge'ez, Sabaean and Greek—never in Amharic.

8-10.　　On these coins, their diffusion and Greek inscriptions, see Richard Pankhurst, "The Greek Coins of Aksum," *Abba Salama* 5 (1975): 70–83.

8-11.　　The belief is that the church was the first place of worship to be erected after the country's conversion to Christianity around 330 AD; was rebuilt by Emperor Fasiladas in the early sixteenth century, after its destruction by the Imam Ahmad ibn Ibrahim's Adal army; and was finally reconstructed by Emperor Iyasu II, in 1750. Pankhurst, *History of Ethiopian Towns,* 180–1.

8-12.　　For a discussion of this and related legends see Roderick Grierson and Stuart Munro-Hay, *The Ark of Covenant* (London, 1999); also Ernest Alfred Thompson Wallis Budge, *The Queen of Sheba and her Only Son Menyelek* (London, 1922), 66–82.

8-13.　　The right of asylum—at Aksum and other religious centres in Ethiopia—was long established, and was supposed to protect all citizens, Muslim as well as Christian, from arrest by the country's secular authorities. Pankhurst, *Social History,* 128, 161, 199–201, 214, 236

8-14.　　Queen Victoria's congratulations had in fact been received some ten days earlier, for Milward's diary for 12 May noted that Napier had been awarded the Grand Cross of the Royal Victorian Order. Chojnacki and Marshall, "Journal," 111.

8-15.　　This church was built "against the side of a perpendicular cliff, several hundred feet high," so that the live rocks formed the back wall. "The front wall [was] covered with rude paintings, damaged by time and damp." In the interior "a carved wooden archway" opened on to the "holy place...rich in crosses and banners, chalices, and old Geez manuscripts." A nearby cavern contained the bones of "three hundred Christian martyrs." Markham. *History,* 185–6.

8-16.　　Simpson is here apparently mistaken. The church, like many others in Ethiopia, was called Debra Libanos after Mount Lebanon. As for the nearby "shrine," it was located in a cavern, said by Markham, *History,* 196, to "contain the bones of St. Romanos." See also Shepherd, *Campaign,* 69.

PART IX: 25 May to 2 June (PAGES 127-135)

9-1.　　These gifts consisted of 6 mortars, 6 howitzers, 725 muskets and 130 fuzils [light muskets], as well as 1,650 pounds of gunpowder, 354,030 rounds of ammunition,

585,480 percussion caps, and a sizable amount of additional equipment and food-stuffs. H & H, *Record,* 11, 96–7. Some of the muskets had been used by the Bombay and Punjab Infantry during the Expedition.

9-2.   Kasa, it is interesting to note, was thus voicing almost exactly the fears which had been expressed by Theodore only a few years earlier. The basic fact was that Ismail Pasha, who became Ottoman governor of Egypt in 1863, had revived the ambitions of his grandfather Muhammad Ali to expand into the Sudan and along the Red Sea coast of Africa, on the borders of Ethiopia. Zewde Gabre-Sellassie, *Yohannes,* 54; Ghada H. Talhmi, *Suakin and Massawa under Egyptian Rule 1865–1885* (Washington, 1979) 19–33.

9-3.   *Tej* was traditionally drunk by the aristocracy.

9-4.   *Chowry,* Anglo-Indian: a fly-whisk, in India often made from the tail of a Tibetan Yak, but in Ethiopia almost invariably of horse-hair. Yule and Burnell, *Hobson-Jobson,* 214–15.

9-5.   *Alga,* Amharic, a bed, but also a throne. *Zufan,* Amharic, a throne, or seat of justice, often superior to an alga. Kane, *Dictionary.*

9-6.   The traveller Henry Dufton, who was working for the Expedition's Intelligence Department. Shepherd, *Campaign,* 340; Markham, *History,* 80, 385–6; H& H, *Record,* II, 101. For an account of Dufton's earlier travels in Ethiopia see his *Narrative* (passim.)

9-7.   Werner Münzinger, a Swiss adventurer, had by then lived in the Ethiopian area for over ten years. He had been put in charge of the British consulate at Massawa in 1865, and subsequently became an adviser and interpreter for the Expedition.

9-8.   His body, according to Shepherd, was "left hanging from a tree close by, a testimony to his guilty associates that the English abhor and will punish the shedding of innocent blood." Shepherd, *Campaign,* 341.

9-9.   The *Queen of the South* was a hospital ship which had sailed from Portsmouth, England and arrived at Annesley Bay on 13 May with 586 tons of medical supplies. It was staffed by 31 men of the Army Hospital Corps.

PART X: 11 June to 2 July (PAGES 136-140)

10-1.   Charles Alleyne Austin (1838–1903), who later reported for *The Times* on the Franco-Prussian war. It is interesting to note that his report of the capture of Magdala reached the British troops in Ethiopia on 2 June, immediately prior to their departure. Chojnacki and Marshall, "Journal," 115.

10-2. Captain Arbuthnot returned to Britain with a *tabot,* which he presented to St. John's Episcopal Church in Edinburgh, Scotland. This was discovered in a cupoard over a century later and returned to Ethiopia, where its restitution was welcomed by thousands of citizens of Addis Ababa. (*The Scotsman,* 28 January 2002; and *Addis Tribune,* 15 February 2002.

10-3.   Alaqa Zannab, the keeper of Téwodros' royal archives, and author of the Emperor's royal chronicle. He was described by Rassam as "a pious Christian," and "an excellent scribe and perfectly trustworthy," so much so that the envoy "never hesitated to confide my secrets to him." Rassam, *Mission*, II, 192–3, 348, For his chronicle of Téwodros see M. M. Moreno, "Cronaca," 143–80. See also Rubenson, *Survival*, 22–4.

10-4.   Speedy later reported that, at about 10 p.m. on the evening of 15 June, he "heard an agonised scream, which was accompanied by a cry for me in Amharic, and which I recognised as proceeding from Alamayou...I found Alamayou in the arms of Lord Napier suffering from the greatest agitation—after quietening with some difficulty his distress, the only solution the boy would give as to the cause of his distress was that Alaca Zarat [sic] had the evil eye!" Zannab, and a servant who had been appointed to look after the prince, were thereupon dismissed, and sent by boat to Mombassa, after which their royal charge passed under Speedy's exclusive control.

This account, which does not appear to have been confirmed by any other witness, was perhaps not fully accepted by Rassam, who merely observes that "for some reason or other, the Alakâ was subsequently discharged, which, if regard be had to the Prince's eventual usefulness to his own country, is much to be regretted." Amulree, "Prince Alamayou," 8–9; Rassam, *Mission,* II, 348.

10-5.   The *Salsotte* was discharged from service with the Expedition on 28 March. It had resumed carrying passengers and mail between Bombay and Suez.

10-6.   Shalaqa Kasa. On his subsequent arrival in Britain, he was photographed, with Alamayou and Speedy, by the notable British photographer Julia Margaret Cameron (1815–1879). This photograph is reproduced in several collections of her works, most recently in T. Powell, *Victorian Photographs of Famous Men and Fair Women* (London, 1973), plate 34.

10-7.   Richard Bickerton Pemell, first Earl Lyons (1817–1887).

10-8.   A plaque in the Chapel reads:

Near this spot lies buried

ALAMAYU

the son of Theodore King of Abyssinia
born 23 April 1861
died 14 November 1879
This tablet is placed to his memory by
QUEEN VICTORIA

"I was a stranger and ye took me in

APPENDIX B [VISISTS TO CHURCHES] (PAGES 145-155)

B-1.   *Makdas*, the central or innermost part of the church, and the place where the *tabot*, or altar slab, is kept. Aymro Wondmagegnehu and Moltovu, *Church*, 46.

  Tabot, Ge'ez and Amharic, an altar slab, sometimes made of stone, but more usually of wood. It was believed to symbolise the Tablets given by God to Moses and/or the Ark of the Covenant. E. Ullendorff, *Ethiopia and the Bible* (London, 1968), 82–9, 122. 2-28. See also Hyatt, *Church*, 121.

B-2.   The following words are common to Ge'ez and Amharic: *Mesraq*, East, or the Orient; *Me'erab*, West, or the Occident; *Debub*, South; *Samen*, North.

B-3.   For an English translation of the Ge'ez legend of the Queen of Sheba's visit to King Solomon, in Jerusalem, and of the birth of her son by the Israeli king, as embodied in the Ethiopian national epic, the *Kebra Nägast*, or Glory of Kings, see Budge, *Queen of Sheba*.

B-4.   On the Falashas and their traditional ignorance of Hebrew, see Steven Kaplan, *The Beta Israel (Falasha) in Ethiopia from Earliest Times to the Twentieth Century* (New York, 1992), 206.

B-5.   Here Simpson is mistaken; Menelik is supposed to have travelled to Jerusalem, not "for his education" but to see Solomon, his father.

B-6.   Simpson here again deviates from the legend, which claims that it was not Menelik who "induced" some priests to accompany him to Ethiopia, but Solomon who ordered the "first-born of Israel" to do so.

B-7.   Simpson is correct in stating that the Ark is traditionally believed to be in Aksum. He is, however, incorrect in stating that the sacred artifact can be seen only by the Abun. The person endowed with this privilege is not the Abun, but a specially appointed guardian.

  Nebula Ed [Ge'ez], is a title given to the head of the principal church of Aksum, that of St. Mary of Zion. He is in no sense the "Keeper of the Ark." Aymro Wondmagegnehu and Moltovu, *Church*, 149.

B-8.   This story about the three obelisks erected by the three sons of Noah is again entirely alien to the standard Sheba and Solomon legend.

B-9.   *Mo'a anbasa za'emenagada Yehuda*, i.e. "The Lion of the Tribe of Judah hath Conquered."

  On these two seals, and the rationale behind them, see Sven Rubenson, "The Lion of the Tribe of Judah, Christian Symbol and/or Imperial Title," *Journal of Ethiopian Studies*, 3 no. 2 (1965): 75–86; Richard Pankhurst, "Letter Writing and the Use of Royal and Imperial Seals in Ethiopia prior to the Twentieth Century," *Journal of Ethiopian Studies*, 11 no. 1 (1973): 179 ff.

B-10.   On these and other themes in Ethiopian art see S. Chojnacki, *Major Themes in Ethiopian Painting* (Wiesbaden 1893).

B-11.   The Ethiopian *sistrum*, in Amharic, *tsanatsel*. Michael Powne, *Ethiopian Music: An Introduction* (London, 1968), 23–4.

  A kettle-drum (in Amharic, *kabaro*) used in religious services. Powne, ibid, 15–18.

SELECT BIBLIOGRAPHY

Abir, Mordechai. *Ethiopia: The Era of the Princes: The Challenge of Islam and the Re-unification of the Christian Empire, 1768-1855.* London, 1968.

Acton, Roger. *The Abyssinian Expedition and the Life and Reign of King Theodore.* London, 1868.

Amulree, Basil William Sholto Mackenzie, Lord. "Prince Alamayou of Ethiopia." *Ethiopia Observer* 8 (1970): 8-15.

Appleyard, David and Arthur Kinlock Irvine. *Letters from Ethiopian Rulers: Early and Mid-Nineteenth Century.* London, 1985.

Appleyard, D. and Richard Pankhurst. "The Last Two Letters of Emperor Tewodros II of Ethiopia (April 11 and 12, 1868)." *Journal of the Royal Asiatic Society* 1 (1986): 23-32.

Archer, Mildred and Paul Theroux. *Visions of India: The Sketchbooks of William Simpson, 1859-1862.* London, 1988.

Arnold, Percy. *Prelude to Magdala: Emperor Theodore of Ethiopia and British Diplomacy.* London, 1992.

Aymro Wondmagegnehu and J. Moltovu. *The Ethiopian Orthodox Church.* Addis Ababa, 1970.

Azene Bekele-Tesemma. *Useful Trees and Shrubs in Ethiopia.* Addis Ababa, 1993.

Bairu Tafla. *Aṣma Giyorgis and His Work: History of the Gāllā and the Kingdom of Šawā.* Stuttgart, 1987.

———. ed. *A Chronicle of Emperor Yoḥannes IV, 1872-89.* Weisbaden, 1977.

Bassano, Francesco (da). *Vocabolario Tegray-Italiano.* Rome, 1918.

Bates, Darrell. "The Abyssinian Boy." *History Today* (December 1979): 816-23.

———. *The Abyssinian Difficulty: The Emperor Theodorus and the Magdala Campaign, 1867-68.* Oxford, 1979.

Bahru Zedwe, *A History of Modern Ethiopia, 1855-1974.* London, 1991.

Baum, Wilhelm. *Die Verwandlungen des Mythos vom Reich des Priestkönigs Johannes.* Flagenfurt, 1999.

Beke, Charles Tilstone. *The British Captives in Abyssinia.* London, 1867.

Blanc, Henry. *A Narrative of Captivity in Abyssinia.* London, 1868.

Blandford, William T. *Observations on the Geology and Zoology of Abyssinia.* London, 1870.

Blundell, Michael *Wild Flowers of East Africa.* London, 1987.

Budge, Ernest Alfred Thompson Wallis. *The Queen of Sheba and her Only Son Menyelek.* London, 1922.

———. *The Book of the Saints of the Ethiopian Church,* 4 vols. Cambridge, 1928.

C. C. [Cornelia Cotton] (Mrs. Speedy). "Anecdotes of Almayu, the Late King Theodore's Son." London, n.d.

Cerulli, Enrico. Etiopi in Palestina: *Storia della communità etiopica di Gerusalemme.* Rome, 1946-1948.

Chandler, D. G. "The Expedition to Abyssinia, 1867-8." In B. Bond, *Victorian Military Campaigns,* 115-59. London, 1967.

Cheesman, Robert Ernest. *Lake Tana and the Blue Nile.* London, 1936.

Chojnacki, Stanislaw. *Major Themes in Ethiopian Painting.* Wiesbaden, 1893.

———. "William Simpson and his journey to Ethiopia, 1868." *Journal of Ethiopian Studies* 6 no. 2 (July 1868): 7-38.

———. and Innes Marshall. "Colonel Milward's Abyssinian Journal: 2 December 1867 to 13 June 1868." *Journal of Ethiopian Studies* 7 no. 1 (1969): 81-118.

Coldham, Geraldine E. *A Bibliography of Scriptures in African Languages.* London, 1966.

Crummey, Donald. "Tewodoros as Reformer and Modernizer." *Journal of African History* 10 (1969): 457-69.

———. "The Violence of Téwodros." *Journal of Ethiopian Studies* 9 no. 2 (1971): 107-25.

———. *Priests and Politicians: Protestant and Catholic Missions in Orthodox Ethiopia, 1830-1868.* Oxford, 1972.

De Cosson, Emelius Albert. *The Cradle of the Blue Nile: A Visit to the Court of King John of Ethiopia.* London, 1877.

Dictionary of National Biography. 1973.

Dufton, Henry. *Narrative of a Journey Through Abyssinia in 1862-3.* London, 1867.

Fanton, Aristide. *L'Abyssinie lors de l'expédition anglaise (1867-1868).* Paris, 1936.

Fine Art Society, *Mr. William Simpson of the Illustrated London News: Pioneer War Artist, 1823-1899.* London, 1987.

Flad, Martin. *60 Jahre in der Mission unter den Falachas.* Giessen and Basel, 1922.

Fusella, Luigi "Le lettere del Dabtarā Assaggākhañ." *Rassegna di Studi Etiopici.* 12 (1953): 80-95; 13 (1953): 20-30.

———. "La cronaca dell' Imperatore Teodoro II di Etiopia in un manoscritto amarico." *Annali dell' Instituto Universitario Orientale di Napoli* 6 (1954-6): 61-121.

Gibbs, F. "Account of the Order of the Cross and Seal of Solomon proposed to have been founded by King Theodore of Abyssinia." *Proceedings of the Bombay Branch of the Royal Asiatic Society* (1889) (unable to obtain further publication information).

Girard, Alexis *Souvenirs d'un voyage en Abyssinie,* 1868-9. Cairo, 1873.

Girma-Selassie Asfaw and David L. Appleyard. *The Amharic Letters of Emperor Theodore of Ethiopia to Queen Victoria and Her Special Envoy.* London. 1979.

Gobat, Samuel. *Journal of Three Years' Residence in Abyssinia.* London, 1834.

Grierson, Roderick and Stuart Munro-Hay. *The Ark of Covenant.* London, 1999.

Guida d'Italia della Consociazione Turistica Italiana. *Africa Orientale Italiana.* Milan, 1938.

Gullick, John Michael. "Captain Speedy of Larut." *Bulletin of the Malayan Branch of the Royal Asiatic Society* 26 no. 3 (1953).

Harrington, Peter. "The first true war artist." *MHQ, The Quarterly Journal of Military History* 9 no. 1 (Autumn 1996).

Henty, George Alfred. *The March to Magdala.* London, 1868.

Holland, Trevenen J. and Henry M. Hozier. *Record of the Expedition to Abyssinia.* 3 vol. London, 1870.

Hooker, J. R. "The Foreign Office and the Abyssinian Captives." *Journal of African History* 2 no. 2 (1961): 245-58.

House of Commons. *Correspondence respecting Abyssinia, 1848-1868.* London, 1868.

———. *Further Papers Connected with the Abyssinian Expedition.* London, 1868.

———. *Parliamentary Record,* 1871.

———. "Memorandum submitted by the Association for the Return of Magdala Ethiopian Treasures (AFROMET)." Culture, Media and Sport Committee, Seventh Report on Cultural Property: Return and Illicit Trade. III: 354-58. London, 2000.

Hozier, Henry M. *The British Expedition to Abyssinia.* London, 1869.

Huntingford, George Wynn Brereton. *The Historical Geography of Ethiopia from the First Century AD to 1704.* London, 1989.

Hyatt, Henry Middleton. *The Church of Abyssinia.* London, 1928.

Illustrated London News. London, 1868. Passim.

Institute of Ethiopian Studies. *Ethiopian Pillows: From the Collections of the Ethnological Museum of the Institute of Ethiopian Studies.* Addis Ababa, 2000.

Isaacs, Albert Augustus. *Life of H. A. Stern.* London, 1886.

Jaenen, Cornelius J. "Theodore II and British Intervention in Ethiopia." *Canadian Journal of History* 1 (1966): 94-151.

Jesman, Czesman. "The Tragedy of Magdala: an Historical Study." *Ethiopia Observer* 10 (1966): 94-151.

Kane, Thomas Lieper. *Amharic-English Dictionary.* Weisbaden, 1990.

Kaplan, Steven. *The Beta Israel (Falasha) in Ethiopia from Earliest Times to the Twentieth Century.* New York, 1992.

Keane, Marcus. *The Towers and Temples of Ireland.* London, 1865.

Kodolitsch, Theodor von. *Die englische Armee in Abyssinien im Feldzug, 1867*

1868. Vienna, 1868.

―――. "Bericht über die englische Armee in Abyssinien, 1867-1868." *Streffleurs österreishische miliärische Zeitschrift* 9 no. 4 (1868): 209-46; 10 no. 1 (1869): 1-48, 161-82, 297-331; 10 no. 2 (1869): 1-16, 65-80, 165-96.

[Kotziga, Yohannes] "Methodios, Metropolitan of Aksum: An Unpublished document edited and translated into English." Abba Salama 1 (1970): 14-66.

Lefebvre, Théophile. *Voyage en Abyssinie,* 6 vol. Paris, 1845-1848.

Lejean, Guillaume. *Voyage en Abyssinie executé de 1862 à 1864.* Paris, 1872.

Leslau, Wolf. *Comparative Dictionary of Ge'ez.* Weisbaden, 1987.

Lindley, Augustus F. *The Abyssinian War from an Abyssinian Point of View.* London, 1868.

Lipscomb, A. H. H. "William Simpson (1823-1899), 'Prince of Pictorial Correspondents.'" 1999.

Ludolf, Hiob. *Nouvelle histoire d'Abissinie ou d'Ethiopie.* Paris, 1684.

―――. New History of Ethiopia. London, 1684.

Markham, Clement Robert. *A History of the Abyssinian Expedition.* London, 1869.

Mondon-Vidailhet, Casimir. *Chronique de ThÈodoros II, roi des rois d'Éthiopie, 1853-1868.* Paris, 1904.

Moorehead, Alan. *The Blue Nile.* New York, 1962.

Moreno, Martino Mario. "La cronaca di re Teodoro attribuita al dabtarà 'Zaneb.'" Rassegna di Studi Etiopici 2 (1942): 143-80.

Morgan, Margaret. "Continuities and Traditions in Ethiopian History: An Investigation of the Reign of Tewodros." *Ethiopia Observer* 12 (1969): 244-92.

Munro-Hay, Stuart. *Aksum: An African Civilisation of Late Antiquity.* Edinburgh, 1991.

Myatt, Frederick. *The March to Magdala: The Abyssinian War, 1868.* London, 1970.

Neugebauer, Otto. *Ethiopic Astronomy and Computus.* Vienna, 1979.

Pankhurst, Richard. "The Emperor Theodore and the question of foreign artisans in Ethiopia." *Boston University Papers on Africa: African History* 2 (1966): 215-35.

―――. *Economic History of Ethiopia, 1800-1935.* Addis Ababa, 1968.

―――. "Linguistic and Cultural Data on the Penetration of Fire-arms into Ethiopia." *Journal of Ethiopian Studies* 9 no. 1 (1971): 47-82.

―――. "Caves in Ethiopian History:Cave Sites in the Environs of Addis Ababa." *Ethiopia Observer* 16 (1973), 15-34.

―――. "Letter Writing and the Use of Royal and Imperial Seals in Ethiopia prior to the Twentieth Century." *Journal of Ethiopian Studies* 11 no. 1 (1973): 179-208.

———. "The Question of a Greco-Romanian or Russian Hermit or Adventurer in Nineteenth Century Ethiopia." *Abba Salama* 5 (1974): 136-59.

———. "The Greek Coins of Aksum." *Abba Salama* 5 (1975): 70-83.

———. "The History of an Ethiopian Icon." *African Affairs* 81 (1982): 117-25.

———. "Captain Speedy's 'Entertainment': The Reminiscences of a Nineteenth Century British Traveller to Ethiopia." *Africa* 38 no. 3 (1983): 428-48.

———. *History of Ethiopian Towns from the Middle Ages to the Early Nineteenth Century.* Stuttgart, 1985.

———. *The History of Famine and Epidemics in Ethiopia Prior to the Twentieth Century.* Addis Ababa, 1985.

———. "Some Brief Notes on the Ethiopian tabot and mänbära tabot." *Quaderni di Studi Etiopici* 8-9 (1987-8): 26-32.

———. *A Social History of Ethiopia.* Addis Ababa, 1990.

———. *History of Ethiopian Towns from the Mid-Nineteenth Century to 1935.* Stuttgart, 1994.

———, ed. and Manoel Barradas. Tractatus *Tres Historico-Geographi (1634): A Seventeenth Century Historical and Geographical Account of Tigray, Ethiopia.* Wiesbaden, 1966.

Pankhurst, Rita. "The Library of Emperor Tewodros II at Mäqdäla (Magdala)." *Bulletin of the School of Oriental and African Studies* 36 no. 1 (1973): 15-42.

Parkyns, Mansfield. *Life in Abyssinia.* London, 1853.

Pearce, Nathaniel. *The Life and Adventures of Nathaniel Pearce.* London, 1831.

Phillipson, David. W. *Ancient Ethiopia. Aksum: Its Antecedents and Successors.* London, 1998.

Plant, Ruth. *The Architecture of the Tigray, Ethiopia.* Worcester, 1985.

Plowden, Walter Chichele. *Travels in Abyssinia and the Galla Country.* London, 1868.

Powell, T. *Victorian Photographs of Famous Men and Fair Women.* London, 1973.

Powne, Michael. *Ethiopian Music: An Introduction.* London, 1968.

Rassam, Hormuzd. *Narrative of the British Mission to Theodore, King of Abyssinia.* London, 1869.

Right, Maria. "The Struggle for a Stronger Ethiopia and the Anglo-Ethiopian War of 1867-1868." In J. Tubiana, *Modern Ethiopia from the Rise of Menelik up to the Present,* 147-57. Nice, 1977.

Rubenson, Sven. "The Lion of the Tribe of Judah, Christian Symbol and/or Imperial Title." *Journal of Ethiopian Studies* 3 no. 2 (1965): 75-85.

———. *King of Kings: Tewodros of Ethiopia.* Addis Ababa, 1966.

———. *The Survival of Ethiopian Independence.* London, 1976.

———. "Takla Giyorgis." In *Dictionary of African Biography.* New York, 1977.

————. *Tewodros and his Contemporaries, 1855-1868*. Addis Ababa and Lund, 1994.

Salt, Henry. *A Voyage to Abyssinia*. London, 1814.

Seckendorff, G. (Graf) von. *Meine Erlebnisse mit dem englischen Expeditions corps in Abessinien, 1867-1868*. Potsdam, 1869.

Sergew Hable Sellassie. *Ancient and Medieval Ethiopian History to 1270*. Addis Ababa, 1972.

————. *Bookmaking in Ethiopia*. Leiden, 1981.

Shepherd, A. F. *The Campaign in Abyssinia*. Bombay, 1868.

Simpson, William. *Illustrations of the War in the East*. London, 1855-6.

————. "An Artist's Jottings in Abyssinia." *Good Words* (1 October 1868): 605-13 (Abbreviated as: "Jottings").

————. "Church Architecture of Abyssinia." *Transactions of the Royal Institute of British Architects*, 1873: 234-46.

————. "Notes and Recollections of my Life." 1892 (Abbreviated as: "Notes").

————. *The Autobiography of William Simpson, R.I.* Edited by G. Eyre-Todd. London, 190. (Abbreviated as: *Autobiography*).

————. "In the trenches before Sebastopol." *English Illustrated Magazine* 14 (December 1895).

————. "Winter and Summer in the trenches before Sebastopol." *English Illustrated Magazine* 15 (April 1896): 33-42.

Slessarev, V. *Prester John: The Letter and the Legend*. Minneapolis, 1959.

Speedy: see C. C. (Cornelia Cotton).

Stanley, Henry Morton. *Coomassie and Magdala: The Story of Two British Campaigns in Africa*. London, 1874.

Stern, Henry Aaron. *Wanderings among the Falashas in Abyssinia: Together with a Description of the Country and its Various Inhabitants*. London, 1862.

————. *The Captive Missionary*. London, 1868.

Taddese Beyene, Richard Pankhurst and Shiferaw Bekele. *Kasa and Kasa: Papers on the Lives, Times and Images of Téwodros II and Yohannes IV (1855 1889)*. Addis Ababa, 1990.

Taddesse Tamrat. *Church and State in Ethiopia, 1270-1527*. Oxford, 1972.

Talhmi, Ghada H. *Suakin and Massawa under Egyptian Rule, 1865-1885*. Washington, 1979.

Theodore's Cattle. Poona, 1869.

Tsegaye Gabre Medhin. "Tewodros: A Play." *Ethiopian Observer* 9 (1965), 209-226.

Ullendorff, Edward. *The Ethiopians: An Introduction to Country and People*. London, 1960.

————. *Ethiopia and the Bible*. London, 1968.

Valentia, George. *Voyages and Travels to India, Ceylon, the Red Sea, Abyssinia, and Egypt*. 1809.

Waldmeier, Theophilus. *The Autobiography of Theophilus Waldmeier, Missionary*. London, 1886.

————. *Erlebnisse in Abessinien*. Basel, 1896.

Walker, Charles Howell. *The Abyssinian At Home*. London, 1933.

Weld Blundell, Herbert. "History of King Theodore." *Journal of the African Society* 6 (1905): 12-42.

Wolde Michael Kelecha. *A Glossary of Ethiopian Plant Names*. Addis Ababa, 1987.

Wylde, Augustus Blande. *Modern Abyssinia*. London, 1901.

Yule, Henry and A. C. Burnell. *Hobson-Jobson*. Calcutta, 1886.

Zewde Gabre-Sellassie. *Yohannes IV of Ethiopia: A Political Biography*. Oxford, 1975.

————. "Webé." In *Dictionary of African Biography*, 146-47. New York, 1977.

İ Π D E X